Chinese Cooking for Everyone
was created, edited and produced by
CFW Publications Limited
130 Connaught Rd Central, Hong Kong
© 1984 Creative Educational Press

EDITORIAL AND PRODUCTION COORDINATOR: Allan Amsel
DESIGN: Alan Chan
FOOD PHOTOGRAPHY: William Wong and Jacki P. Bennett
CHINESE CALIGRAPHY: Jat See Yeu

First published in the USA 1984 by Gallery Books
An imprint of W. H. Smith Publishers Inc
112 Madison Avenue, New York, New York 10016

Library of Congress Cataloging in Publication Data
ISBN: 0 8317 1247-3

Printed in Hong Kong

ChineseCooking ForEveryone

110 Authentic Chinese Family Dishes

GALLERY BOOKS
An Imprint of W. H. Smith Publishers Inc.
112 Madison Avenue
New York City 10016

Contents

The Recipes: Around the Regions of China

To the purist, the various styles of Chinese food can be innumerable, representing not just every province of China but geographical and even tribal divisions within provinces. In recent years, however, regional cooking — spreading rapidly throughout the world in ever more authentic forms — has been broken down by gourmets into four basic categories: Southern, Northern, Eastern and Western. We have divided the recipes in this book into these practical categories.

We start with the Southern, the most familiar to us, taking in food from the province of Kwangtung (whose capital is Canton), and also the food of Swatow and Hainan. Here the emphasis is on the easy stir-fry cooking, using pork, chicken, seafoods and vegetables to achieve delicate, refreshing tastes. We move to the North, covering Pekinese food with its hint of the Mongolian influence. Northern meals, you will find, are hearty and well flavoured. Next we move on to the East, to food from the great port city of Shanghai and the coastal province of Fukien, where we encounter stronger seasonings for a robust cuisine that, unlike the other cooking of China, tends to be high in calories. We wind up in the West, concentrating on the intensely spicy food of Szechwan, where chillies and garlic add a searing taste. This is rapidly becoming one of the most popular ethnic cuisines in the West.

As you master the relatively simple and easy to follow recipes listed on these pages, you will not only be on your way to becoming a skilled Chinese home cook, but also one who is unusually cosmopolitan.

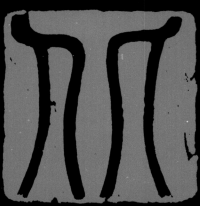

Eastern:

52. Cubed Fish with Broccoli
Barbecue Sauce Fish
54. Braised Yellow Fish
Abalone with Oyster Sauce
Clams in Bean Sauce
56. "Drunk Chicken"
Chicken Wrapped in Paper
Walnut Chicken
58. Sweet and Sour Duck with
Ginger
Braised Brown Sauce Duck
Lion's Head Meatballs
60. Crisp Fried Pork Chops
Braised Spareribs
Beef in Barbecue Sauce
62. Oyster Sauce Beef
Braised Beef with Beancurd
and Vegetables
Bean Salad

64. Chop Suey Chicken
Baby Corn and Mushrooms
Cabbage in Cream Sauce
66. Braised Vegetables with
Beancurd
Shanghai Noodles with
Beanshoots

Western:

68. Fish in Hot Tomato Sauce
Westlake Fish
70. Szechwan Chilli Prawns
Spiced Chicken
Stir-Fried Chicken with
Beanshoots and Hot
Peppers
72. Szechwan Diced Chicken
"Ma Po" Minced Pork with
Beancurd
Twice-Cooked Garlic Pork
74. Simmered Pork
Barbecued Spareribs
Szechwan Stewed Beef
76. Chilli Beef with Vegetables
Garlic Steaks
Sweet and Sour Cabbage
Salad
78. Quick Fry Spinach

Shrimps in Tomato Sauce on
Popped Rice Cakes
80. Combination Chow Mein
Beef on Crisp Noodles

Dim Sims and Snacks:

82. Golden Shrimp Balls
Prawn Toast
84. Spring Rolls
Pork Dim Sums
Deep-Fried Wonton
85. Fried Crab Claws

Soups:

86. Golden Sweetcorn Soup
Clear Mushroom Soup
Winter Melon Soup
87. Combination Long Soup
88. Chicken, Vegetable and Egg
Soup
Wonton Soup with Meat and
Vegetables
Fish Ball and Celery Soup

Sweets:

90. Lychees in Syrup
Double-Boiled Pineapple and
Pawpaw
Almond Jelly with Fruit
92. Toffied Apple and Banana

Seafood

Poultry

Pork

Beef

Lamb

Vegetables & Egg

Rice & Noodles

Introduction: Chinese Family Dining

It was the food of the Southern Cantonese that first reached other parts of the world. The great gold rush days brought an influx of Chinese fortune seekers to Australia, and where a Chinese goes, so too does his *Wok* and soy sauce. For with these, he can prepare, using whatever ingredients are to hand, meals which if not ideal, at least reflect the ideals of this great cuisine.

Availability of ingredients (or lack of it) quite obviously affected the food, and the style of Chinese cooking which we grew up with was one unique to Australia. One of bland, watery sauces, a hotchpotch of vegetables tasting predominently of celery and bamboo shoots with the merest hint of meat; of black bean sauces and of heavy 'dim sims'.

But in recent years a serious interest in ethnic cuisines from all parts of the world, coupled with an upsurge in immigration from Asia, has found us with virtually every type of Chinese cooking ingredient on sale in major cities, and even in the country towns basic products are readily obtainable.

Today we do not merely enjoy Chinese food, the consumption of which in restaurants, from take-away counters and that cooked in the home, far exceeds any other type of imported cuisine in Australia. We are learning to discriminate between regional cooking styles, and to demand quality, not merely quantity as we did in the past.

Yet our increased awareness of the sophisticated pleasures Chinese food has to offer should not lead to the misconception that real Chinese cooking is something to be entrusted only to a master chef who has served a long apprenticeship. For close to a billion of the world's population, this most variegated and refined of all the world's cuisines, is looked upon as ordinary home cooking — save for a token number of special dishes which need the large-scale production area of a restaurant for their preparation.

Fine Chinese cooking is something you can accomplish with a little practice, and with little or no special equipment in your kitchen. Above all, it is now one of the most inexpensive ways to produce nourishing, tasty meals at home.

Approach Chinese cooking with an open mind. Be ready to put aside some, though hardly all, of the principles you have always accepted when dealing with Western cooking. Since the process of cooking is most often an extremely fast one, of equal importance to the actual cooking then, is the preparation of ingredients, including the seasonings, before cooking begins.

This matter of careful and complete preparation and the various most used cooking methods, is dealt with in the following pages. Whether or not you have already attempted to cook Chinese food, it would be well to study the basics of preparation before plunging into the specific recipes.

As for the question of the philosophy behind the cooking, this, for your practical purposes, is nothing difficult or esoteric. It means no more than keeping the concept of balance and harmony uppermost in your mind. Harmony of flavours, textures and colours, and a balance between the opposing factors of staple — either rice bread or pasta — and meat, poultry, seafood and vegetables.

As you advance, you will begin to compile your own menus with these recipes, becoming more flexible and imaginative in your selection. The basic guideline of balance and harmony should help you in your choice of dishes to be served together.

As all Chinese dishes are intended to be served with other main dishes to make up a meal, the question of how many a single dish might serve becomes complicated. As a general rule, each of these recipes could make a light meal for four served with rice or noodles on the side. Therefore to serve six, say, cook two dishes and serve a staple or perhaps a soup.

Before You Start

Because a majority of Chinese dishes are fast-cooked, you will find that a certain amount of your time, during the meal, will have to be spent in the kitchen.

However, this will be for the purpose of actually cooking the meal — something which should take no longer than 5 minutes — the preparation being completed well in advance of cooking time. *Everything* needed for a dish should be placed within reaching distance of the stove before you begin; because when you actually start cooking there will be no time to look for that missing ingredient — at least not without spoiling the dish.

All vegetables and meats are to be cut into pieces small enough to be picked up with chopsticks and each making no more than a single mouthful. The ingredients for any one dish should be of uniform size, both for the matter of even cooking and for appearance. Meats are often chopped into bite-sized pieces, cutting right through the bone. This tends to make them difficult to eat, so if preferred meat, especially poultry, can be de-boned first. Certain braised or steamed meat or poultry dishes have the joint or bird cooked whole. To facilitate eating, the meat should be sliced or chopped into bite-sized pieces before serving, or should be cooked so tender that it can be pulled off in slivers with chopsticks.

Let us look now at some key aspects of preparation, before we move to the stove:

Meat Carving
Most meat dishes require near paper-thin slices which will become supremely tender and absorb a good deal of seasoning, during fast-cooking. The meat should be well chilled, even partially frozen to facilitate cutting, and it should be cut across the grain. This ensures that there will be no long, tough sinews or fibres to spoil the tenderness. Some recipes call for "strips", which should be about 5cm (2") to 7.5cm (3") long and about 1.25cm (½") wide. Others require shreds which are made by cutting thin slices into minute slivers resembling coarse minced meat.

The Basic Marinades
The other secret to the tenderness of meat in Chinese cooking is in the marination. All cooks, from the most renowned master-chefs to housewives soak their sliced or shredded meat in aromatic mixtures of seasoning ingredients which soften the fibres, as well as saturate with flavour.

To simplify your cooking life, here are three that can be used whenever marinades are called for in the recipes that follow. They can be prepared in advance and stored in screw-top jars in the refrigerator.

Meat Marinade
(Makes about 1 cup)
3 tablespoons vegetable oil
3 tablespoons water
2½ tablespoons dry sherry
2 tablespoons light soy sauce

8

1 tablespoon dark soy sauce
1½ teaspoons sesame oil (optional)
1 teaspoon salt
2½ teaspoons sugar
½ teaspoon white pepper
8 slices fresh ginger, minced
2 cloves garlic, peeled

Poultry Marinade
(Makes about ½ cup)
3 tablespoons vegetable oil
3 tablespoon dry sherry
1½ teaspoons salt
3 teaspoons sugar
¾ teaspoon white pepper
4 slices fresh ginger, minced
½ clove garlic, peeled

Seafood Marinade
(Makes about ¼ cup)
3 tablespoons dry sherry
½ teaspoon salt
1½ teaspoons sugar
¼ teaspoon white pepper
8 slices fresh ginger, minced

To prepare marinades, measure ingredients into screw-top jars. Shake well and keep refrigerated until needed.

Vegetable Cutting
Unless otherwise stated in the separate recipes, when *dicing* vegetables, cut them into small cubes about the size of large green peas. *Small dice* will be cut into even more minute cubes. To *shred* vegetables, cut them into slices as thin as you can manage, then cut again into narrow strips.

Carrots or bamboo shoots can be cut into thin discs, strips, or into thin sticks about the size of matchsticks. One traditional method you might like to try, especially with carrots, is a *rolling cut*: first cut diagonally, then roll the vegetable through 180 degrees and cut along the same angle to get triangular shaped pieces.

With such stem vegetables as celery and the stalks of Chinese cabbage, you should cut diagonally, whether cutting into thick or thin slices, so that the greatest possible area will be exposed to the heat and seasonings.

If using canned vegetables, particularly bamboo shoots, water chestnuts or mushrooms, be sure to drain them well. Never use those that come packed in a flavoured sauce, unless specified in the recipe.

Special Ingredients
Those of you who are attempting to cook Chinese food for the first time will encounter certain essential ingredients which might be either unfamiliar to you, or for which you might wish to use a more familiar substitute. In the back of this book, on pages 94-95 we have included a simple glossary of ingredients which covers methods of storage and possible substitutes for many of the most commonly used Chinese ingredients.

Weights and Measures
On page 95 you will find details of measurements used in this book, with a conversion chart should you have not yet updated your measuring equipment.

When You Cook

Although most of your time will go into the preparation, the enjoyment comes in the cooking. Again, there are some key differences between the Chinese and Western approaches. Here now are some matters that will be of concern once the ingredients are ready.

Special Equipment

You could go on forever collecting special Chinese cooking utensils, but the basic needs are few, and can even be done without at a pinch.

You will probably already have the traditional Chinese rounded multi-purpose *Wok*. The cast iron type is the best, though there are excellent ones with teflon lining, and even a flat-bottomed one to go on your electric stove. An iron *Wok* should be carefully broken in by giving it a thorough rubbing with an oiled cloth after scrubbing and heating. After each use, brush it clean, rinse and leave to dry, then rub with an oiled cloth.

If you don't yet have a wok, never mind; go ahead with your most trusty large frying pan.

Life will also be easier if you purchase the inexpensive *Charn*, the small metal shovel used to stir and move foods in the *Wok*. You will probably also want to get yourself a ladle, one more shallow than a soup ladle, for adding liquid ingredients, and to use as a convenient measuring spoon when you advance with your Chinese cooking.

In addition, the sharp rectangular bladed cleaver, a carbon steel one, if possible, is indispensible. Used with the traditional soft-grained chopping board, they make every form of cutting, chopping and slicing easier.

These are the items you might start with, and you may search out a supplier of such additional bits and pieces as bamboo steaming baskets and steaming racks as your skills advance.

Special Techniques
Stir-Frying

Since the majority of Chinese dishes are fast-cooked, meaning for only one to three minutes, you will naturally have to master the stir-fry technique. It is very simple. The method entails pouring a few tablespoons of oil into a *Wok* over intense heat. When the oil begins to smoke, the ingredients are tossed in, the heat reduced very slightly and the ingredients are turned constantly and moved around in the pan. This fast cooking over high heat must be controlled so that the heat seals the surface of the food without overcooking it, locking in essential goodness, moisture and natural tastes.

It is most successfully accomplished over

gas, but if your stove is electric you can, with practice, learn to control the cooking temperature by moving the pan on and off the cooking ring, which is kept at a high temperature.

For best results, stir-frying should be done over *intensely high* heat. Most domestic cookers do not provide the high degree of heat obtainable from a commercial cooker designed for use with a *Wok*. So we have, in some instances, recommended that meats be initially deep-fried to ensure the retention of natural juices and tenderness. However, for convenience and economy, you may choose to stir-fry.

Stir-fried dishes should be served just as quickly as possible after they are cooked.

Steaming

This technique, so popular in Chinese cookery, is usually accomplished in a large *Wok*, covered with a dome-shaped lid, with a wire or bamboo rack placed in the bottom to support the plate containing the food. Heat should be moderate, just enough to maintain a good amount of steam without boiling over or boiling dry. If you don't yet have a *Wok*, or you're using it for other dishes, any saucepan large enough to hold a plate and stand will do.

Stewing

For absolute tenderness and a unique rich taste, whole pieces of meat are often slow-cooked. A heavy casserole or saucepan will give better results than a *Wok* for this; and a crockpot could also be used. This method is called 'red cooking' because plenty of seasoning ingredients, especially soy sauce, are used and these give the meat a deep red-brown colour.

Rice Cooking:

This can be a simple operation following the method most often used by the Chinese. Allow about 60g/2 oz of short grained white rice per person. Wash it once and cover with cold water to a depth of one finger joint (about 2.5cm/1″). Cover and bring to boil on a high heat, then reduce heat to the lowest possible register or use an asbestos mat under the saucepan. Cook for around 18 minutes. For best results use a heavy based aluminium saucepan or a stoneware casserole.

Serving:

For maximum appeal, garnish dishes attractively using the suggestions we have given with each recipe. Serve on round or oval plates or in shallow dishes. Cold dishes are usually served first followed by perhaps a vegetable and seafood dish, then the soup, remaining dishes and sweets or fresh fruit. Rice or noodles may be served early in the meal and eaten right through.

From the South

The most important characteristic of food from the Southern regions of China is freshness. Fish are straight from the sea or river, vegetables are garden-fresh and seasonings subtle to highlight the natural tastes.

The emphasis is on seafoods, coupled with vegetables. Beef is rarely eaten, with pork considered a vastly superior meat as it so easily adapts to the many cooking methods and its bland taste responds well to traditional seasonings. Chicken, too, is popular. Most dishes are stir-fried, and contain a mixture of main ingredients; even blending meat with fish, seafoods or eggs. Stir-Fried Abalone, Mushrooms and Eggs is a good example of the Southern tendency to emphasise more than one main ingredient in a dish.

Dishes from the South are the ones which originally found their way to Western countries, perhaps primarily because little in the way of special sauces and seasonings was needed to produce a reasonable imitation of the real thing.

Presentation and appearance of the food is important. Therefore a good cook will aim, firstly, at combining ingredients which contrast visually and will ensure that they are cut into uniform sizes for each dish. Fresh herbs, tomato flowers and ornate cutouts of animals, fish and a host of other shapes are made from carrot, radish or cucumber and used to decorate the dishes. Additionally fruit, pineapple in particular, may find its way into a dish in combination with meat, or will be used as an edible garnish.

Steamed Whole Fish ▶

625g (1¼ lb) bream, flounder or mullet
1 tablespoon dry sherry
½ teaspoon salt
1 tablespoon light soy sauce
1 tablespoon water
1 tablespoon vegetable oil
8 slices fresh ginger
3 shallots (or 1 medium onion)

Preparation:
Clean fish and wash well. Wipe dry and score diagonally across each side. Place on a fireproof plate and sprinkle with sherry and salt. Rub in lightly, then pour on soy sauce, water and oil.
Shred ginger and shallots and scatter over the fish, pushing some into the cavity.
Leave for 10 minutes.

Cooking:
Heat a pot of water large enough to hold the plate and set a rack or stand inside. When boiling, put in the plate, cover tightly and steam over moderate heat until the fish is tender, approximately 10 minutes. Meat should be just lifting from the bones.

Serving:
Serve the fish on the same plate, adding sprigs of fresh coriander or parsley.

Fish in Sweet Corn Sauce ▶

500g (1¼ lb) meaty white fish fillets
¾ cup cornflour
1 shallot
2 egg whites
deep-frying oil
Sauce:
1 cup cream-style sweetcorn
¾ cup water
1 teaspoon chicken stock powder
2 teaspoons light soy sauce
½ teaspoon salt
2 teaspoons cornflour

Preparation:
Cut fish into 2.5cm (1″) cubes and place in a plastic bag with the cornflour. Shake the bag vigorously to coat fish thickly with flour.
Mix sauce ingredients in a small saucepan, adding finely chopped shallot.
Lightly beat egg whites.

Cooking:
Heat deep-frying oil to very hot in a wok or deep saucepan. Reduce heat slightly and put in the fish pieces. Deep-fry to a light golden brown, about 3 minutes. Lift out and drain well.
Bring sauce to the boil, stirring until thickened. Remove from the heat and slowly pour in the beaten egg white. Do not stir until the egg has set in white threads in the sauce.

Serving:
Place the fried fish cubes in a serving dish and pour on the piping hot sauce. Garnish with finely chopped shallot, and serve with soy sauce.

Ginger Crab

1 large raw mud crab (or 2 small crabs)
5cm (2") piece fresh ginger
1 tablespoon light soy sauce
1 tablespoon dry sherry
1 teaspoon sugar
pinch of salt
4 tablespoons vegetable oil
Sauce:
¼ cup water
½ teaspoon chicken stock powder
2 teaspoons cornflour

Preparation:
Remove claws and crack shells, using the back of a cleaver. Break away undershell and remove mouth, stomach and spongy 'fingers'. Rinse with cold water. Chop into large pieces. Arrange on a fireproof plate. Shred ginger and scatter over the crabs, adding soy sauce, sherry, sugar and salt. Mix sauce ingredients in a bowl.

Cooking:
Set crab in a steamer over rapidly boiling water, cover and steam for 10 minutes. Remove from the steamer and drain off any liquid, and reserve.
Heat oil in a wok and stir-fry crab on high heat for 2 minutes. Add reserved seasonings and the sauce and stir-fry until the sauce thickens and glazes the crab.

Serving:
Arrange on a serving plate and garnish with sprigs of parsley, slices of lemon and preserved ginger.

Stir-Fried Abalone, Mushrooms and Eggs ▶

150g (5 oz) canned abalone, drained
150g (5 oz) canned straw mushrooms, drained
6 dried black mushrooms, soaked
6 small chicken eggs
2 shallots (or 1 small onion)
4 slices fresh ginger
8 fresh lettuce leaves
2 tablespoons vegetable oil
Sauce:
⅔ cup water
2 teaspoons chicken stock powder
1 teaspoon light soy sauce
1 teaspoon dry sherry
1 teaspoon sesame oil
½ teaspoon sugar
2 teaspoons cornflour

Preparation:
Slice abalone very thinly, horizontally. Cut straw mushrooms in halves. Squeeze water from soaked mushrooms, remove stems and shred caps.
Hard-boil eggs, drain and cover with cold water.
Cut shallots into 2.5cm (1") pieces, or slice onion. Shred ginger and wash lettuce in cold water. Drain. Mix sauce ingredients in a bowl.

Cooking:
Heat oil in a wok and when very hot, stir-fry onions and ginger briefly. Add mushrooms and stir-fry on high heat for 2 minutes, then add the abalone and sauce and bring to the boil.
Simmer for 2 minutes, then add the shelled eggs, halved, and stir gently until glazed with the sauce. Remove from the heat.
Bring a pot of water to the boil, add 1 tablespoon vegetable oil and a pinch of salt. Dip in lettuce leaves for about 15 seconds. Drain.

Serving:
Arrange lettuce on a serving plate and pour the abalone, egg and mushroom combination on top.
Sprinkle with a little extra sesame oil.

Prawns Baked in Salt

12 giant raw prawns, in shells
1 kg (2 lb) coarse sea salt

Preparation:
Wash prawns and wipe dry. Do not remove shells. Place a thick layer of salt in a baking tray and arrange the prawns on top. Cover with more salt.

Cooking:
Place the tray in a preheated hot oven and cook for 10-15 minutes, depending on the size of the prawns.

Serving:
Brush off the salt and place prawns on a plate of shredded lettuce, or on paper napkins.
Serve with small bowls of light soy sauce spiked with sliced fresh red chilli.

500 g (1 lb) raw shrimps, peeled
1 tablespoon oil
2 egg whites
1½ tablespoons seafood marinade
125 g (¼ lb) rice stick noodles
60 g (2 oz) fresh beanshoots
½ each green and red peppers
1 stick celery
2 shallots
4 slices fresh ginger
deep-frying oil
Sauce:
¼ cup water
¾ teaspoon chicken stock powder
1 tablespoon light soy sauce
2 teaspoons dry sherry
1 teaspoon sugar
1 teaspoon cornflour
pinch each salt and white pepper

Preparation:
Pound shrimp with the side of a cleaver, or in a mortar, until reduced to a sticky pulp. Add oil, egg whites and season with the marinade. Knead to a smooth paste. To form into balls, squeeze the mixture from a clenched fist, out between curled thumb and forefinger. Scrape off each ball with a spoon and drop into iced water.
When all are done, place in a large pot of boiling, slightly salted water and simmer on moderate heat until they rise to the surface, then cook for 2 more minutes.
Lift out, drain and leave to cool.
Rinse beanshoots and drain. Remove roots and pods, if preferred. Finely shred peppers, celery, shallots and ginger.
Arrange the rice stick noodles in a large wire strainer, and use another strainer, slightly smaller, to press down on the noodles, making a nest shape.

Cooking:
Heat deep-frying oil in a large wok or deep saucepan and when very hot, reduce heat slightly. Hold the strainer in the oil until the "nest" is crisp and a light golden colour. Ensure the complete nest is submerged in the oil. Lift out, drain and place on absorbent paper.
Reheat deep oil and fry shrimp balls to a light golden colour, lift out and drain.
Pour off all but 2 tablespoons oil and fry vegetables on high heat for 1 minute. Add premixed sauce ingredients and bring to the boil. Simmer, stirring, until the sauce thickens. Return the shrimp balls and stir until glazed with the sauce.

Serving:
Place the "nest" on a serving plate and surround with finely shredded lettuce or parsley sprigs. Encircle with alternate slices of tomato and cucumber.
Pile the shrimp "eggs" and vegetables into the "nest".

Sea Scallops with Snowpeas

375g (¾ lb) fresh sea scallops, removed from shells
1 tablespoon seafood marinade
1 leek (or 3 shallots)
125g (¼ lb) fresh snow peas
90g (3 oz) canned straw mushrooms, drained
6 slices fresh ginger
3 tablespoons vegetable oil
Sauce:
⅓ cup water
1 teaspoon chicken stock powder
2 teaspoons light soy sauce
2 teaspoons dry sherry
¾ teaspoon sesame oil (optional)
1 teaspoon cornflour
pinch each of salt and white pepper

Preparation:
Wash scallops, in cold, slightly salted water. Pat dry. Season with marinade and leave for 7 minutes.
Cut leeks into thin diagonal slices and rinse with plenty of cold water, or cut shallots into 2.5cm (1") pieces.
Rinse snow peas, remove strings. Cut mushrooms in halves. Mix sauce ingredients in a bowl.

Cooking:
Heat oil in a wok and when very hot stir-fry leek or shallots for ½ minute. Add snow peas and stir-fry for about ½ minute, then add mushrooms, ginger and scallops and stir-fry on high heat for 1 minute.
Reduce heat slightly and continue cooking, stirring constantly, until scallops are firm and white, about 1½ more minutes. Pour in the sauce and simmer until it thickens and clears.

Serving:
Garnish the dish with tomato wedges and season with a little more sesame oil and white pepper.

Stir-Fried Shrimps, Peas and Cashews

375 g (¾ lb) raw shrimps, peeled
1 tablespoon seafood marinade
1 egg white
2 teaspoons cornflour
60 g (2 oz) frozen green peas
90 g (3 oz) raw cashew nuts
2 shallots
4 slices fresh ginger
1 teaspoon sugar
½ teaspoon sesame oil
pinch each salt and white pepper
deep-frying oil
Sauce:
¼ cup water
1 teaspoon chicken stock powder
½ teaspoon cornflour

Preparation:
Wash shrimps and pat dry. Season with marinade and add beaten egg white and cornflour. Mix well and leave for 10 minutes.
Place peas in a strainer and pour on boiling water to thaw. Drain well. Chop shallots and shred ginger.
Mix sauce ingredients in a bowl.

Cooking:
Heat deep oil to very hot in a wok. Put cashews in a wire strainer or perforated ladle and place in the oil. Fry to a light golden brown, lift out and drain on absorbent paper. Add shrimps to the oil and fry until pink, about ½ minute. Drain. Pour off all but 2 tablespoons oil and fry shallots and ginger for ½ minute. Add peas and stir-fry on high heat for 1½ minutes.
Return shrimps to the pan and season with sugar, sesame oil, salt and pepper. Stir briefly, then pour in the sauce. Bring to the boil and simmer until the sauce thickens and clears. Add cashews and mix well.

Serving:
Garnish with slivers of thinly sliced red chilli and sprigs of parsley.

Sweet and Sour Prawns

500 g (1 lb) raw prawns, peeled
2 tablespoons seafood marinade
2 eggs, separated
cornflour
3 shallots (or 1 medium onion)
½ each green and red peppers
45 g (1½ oz) preserved Chow Chow or Chinese pickles
deep-frying oil
Sauce:
½ cup water
2 tablespoons tomato paste
½ cup white vinegar
90 g (3 oz) brown sugar
4 slices fresh ginger, shredded
2 teaspoons cornflour
pinch of salt
few drops red food colouring (optional)

Preparation:
Rinse prawns and pat dry. Slit down centre backs and scrape out dark veins. Season with marinade. Add lightly beaten egg whites and about 2 teaspoons cornflour, mix well and leave for 10 minutes.
Shred shallots or onion, peppers and Chow Chow or pickles, if the pieces are large.
Mix sauce ingredients in a bowl.
Place about ¾ cup cornflour in a plastic bag. Lightly beat egg yolks and mix with the prawns, then drop into the bag. Shake vigorously to thickly coat prawns with the flour.

Cooking:
Heat deep oil in a wok. Reduce heat slightly when oil is very hot. Shake excess cornflour from prawns and place in the oil. Fry for 1½ minutes, then lift out and drain. Leave to cool slightly, then return to reheated oil and deep-fry for ½ minute more. Drain well. Pour off all but 2 tablespoons oil and fry shallots or onion for ½ minute, on moderately high heat. Add peppers and fry briefly, then add sauce and bring to the boil. When bubbling, add the Chow Chow or pickles and their liquid and cook on moderate heat until sauce has thickened slightly and become clear. Tint with a little food colouring, if used.
Add prawns, and stir to coat with the sauce. Heat through.

Serving:
Arrange prawns on a plate with the vegetables and garnish with finely chopped shallot or parsley.

Note:
For extra flavour, prepare the sauce several hours in advance and reheat before serving, but do not fry the prawns until ready to serve.

Pineapple and Lychee Chicken, page 20 ▶

Pineapple and Lychee Chicken

500 g (1 lb) chicken pieces
1 tablespoon poultry marinade
2 egg whites
¾ cup cornflour
2 cloves garlic (optional)
4 rings canned pineapple
12 canned lychees
2 shallots
deep-frying oil
Sauce:
¼ cup water
1 teaspoon chicken stock powder
¼ cup pineapple juice
2 tablespoons Hoisin sauce
½ teaspoon white vinegar
1 teaspoon sugar
½ teaspoon salt
2 teaspoons cornflour

Preparation:
Chop chicken into bite-sized pieces and season with marinade. Leave for 20 minutes. Mix egg whites with cornflour, adding a little cold water, if needed, to make a thickish batter. Chop garlic, if used. Dice pineapple, drain lychees, cut shallots into small pieces. Mix sauce ingredients in a bowl.

Cooking:
Heat deep oil to very hot, then reduce heat slightly.
Coat chicken pieces with the batter and place one by one in the hot oil. Fry to a deep golden brown, then remove and drain well. Pour off all but 3 tablespoons oil and stir-fry garlic and shallots for 1 minute. Pour in the sauce and bring to the boil. Add chicken, pineapple and lychees and cook until the sauce thickens and becomes clearer.

Serving:
Spoon into a serving dish and garnish with parsley or mint.

Chicken with Almonds and Celery ▶

500 g (1 lb) chicken, boneless
2 tablespoons poultry marinade
2 egg whites
1½ tablespoons cornflour
90 g (3 oz) blanched almonds
2 stalks celery
3 shallots (or 1 small onion)
3 slices fresh ginger
2 cloves garlic (optional)
deep-frying oil
Sauce:
¼ cup water
1 teaspoon chicken stock powder
1 tablespoon light soy sauce
2 teaspoons dry sherry
¾ teaspoon sugar
1 teaspoon cornflour

Preparation:
Cut well-chilled chicken into thin slices, then into shreds. Season with marinade, then mix in cornflour, and egg whites, lightly beaten. Mix well and leave for 20 minutes. Wipe celery and cut into thin diagonal slices. Shred shallots, or slice onion. Shred ginger and chop garlic, if used.
Mix sauce ingredients in a bowl.

Cooking:
Heat deep oil to very hot, then reduce heat slightly. Deep-fry almonds until golden. Drain. Add chicken pieces and deep-fry for ½ minute. Drain.
Pour off all but 3 tablespoons oil and fry celery, onion, ginger and garlic together for 1½ minutes. Add the sauce and bring to the boil. Return chicken and simmer until sauce thickens and clears. Stir in fried almonds.

Serving:
Garnish with tomato wedges and sprigs of parsley.

Chicken and Sweet Potato Casserole

500 g (1 lb) chicken pieces
2 tablespoons poultry marinade
375 g (¾ lb) sweet potato or taro, peeled
2 shallots
4 slices fresh ginger
1 clove garlic
¾ cup thick coconut milk
1 tablespoon cornflour
1½ teaspoons sugar
¾ teaspoon salt
deep-frying oil
Sauce:
1½ cups water
2 teaspoons chicken stock powder
1 tablespoon light soy sauce

Preparation:
Wash chicken and cut into bite-sized pieces. Season with marinade and leave for 20 minutes.
Cut sweet potato or taro into 1.25cm (½") slices.
Cut shallots into 2.5cm (1") pieces. Shred ginger and chop garlic. Mix coconut milk with cornflour, sugar and salt and set aside.

Cooking:
Heat deep oil to very hot and deep-fry sliced sweet potato or taro until lightly coloured, about 4 minutes. Place in a casserole. Deep-fry chicken until lightly coloured and place on the sweet potato or taro in the casserole. Pour off all but 2 tablespoons oil and stir-fry shallots, ginger and garlic for about ½ minute. Add to the casserole and pour in the sauce ingredients.
Cover, place on high heat and bring to the boil. Reduce heat to low and simmer until chicken and potato are cooked through. Stir in the premixed coconut liquid and heat until thickened, but do not allow to boil.

Serving:
Serve in the casserole or transfer to a deep serving dish and garnish with slivers of fresh red chilli.

Sweet and Sour Pork with Pineapple, page 22 ▶

Sweet and Sour Pork with Pineapple

500 g (1 lb) pork tenderloin
2 egg whites
2 tablespoons cornflour
2 tablespoons water
pinch each of salt and bicarbonate of soda
1 large onion
1 green pepper
1 fresh red chilli
1 fresh pineapple
deep-frying oil
Sauce:
¼ cup water
½ cup pineapple juice
1 tablespoon tomato sauce
1 teaspoon Chinese plum sauce
1 tablespoon white vinegar
2 teaspoons sugar
¼ fresh red chilli, minced
3 slices fresh ginger, minced
2 teaspoons cornflour
1 tablespoon vegetable oil

Preparation:
Cut pork into 2.5cm (1″) cubes. Place in a bowl with egg whites, cornflour, water, salt and bicarbonate of soda. Mix well and leave for 20-25 minutes.
Cut onion and green pepper into 2cm (¾″) squares. Shred chilli. Cut pineapple in halves and scoop out flesh. Cut pineapple flesh into small cubes. Set the pineapple shells on a serving plate and surround with shredded lettuce or cabbage. Set aside.
Mix sauce ingredients in a small saucepan.

Cooking:
Bring sauce to the boil, reduce heat and simmer for 4-5 minutes. Keep warm.
Heat deep oil in a large wok and when very hot, reduce heat slightly and deep-fry pork for 3 minutes. Drain and leave to cool.
Blanch onion and green pepper in boiling water for 20 seconds. Drain and splash with cold water. Drain well.
Reheat the oil and fry pork for a second time until lightly browned, with surface well crisped. Drain well.
Place onion and peppers in a strainer and deep-fry for a few seconds. Drain. Pour off all but 2 tablespoons oil and return meat to the pan with onion, peppers, chilli and pineapple cubes. Stir-fry for 1 minute, then pour in the sauce and bring to the boil.

Serving
Spoon pork, vegetables and sauce into the pineapple shells. Garnish with parsley or mint.

Cantonese Spareribs

500 g (1 lb) lean pork spareribs, trimmed
½ cup light soy sauce
2 tablespoons dry sherry
2 tablespoons sugar
2 cloves garlic, crushed
1 tablespoon vegetable oil

Preparation:
Separate ribs and place in a flat dish. Mix the remaining ingredients together and pour over the ribs. Leave for about 6 hours to marinate.

Cooking:
Drain, reserving the marinade, and arrange on a lightly oiled baking tray. Cook under a moderate grill until well browned. Brush with the reserved marinade occasionally. Cook for approximately 15 minutes, turning several times.

Serving:
Arrange the ribs on a plate of shredded lettuce and garnish with cucumber and tomato slices. Serve with a bowl of spicy tomato or chilli sauce.

Plum Sauce Pork

500 g (1 lb) pork tenderloin
1 tablespoon Chinese plum sauce or plum jam
4 tablespoons vegetable oil
Seasoning:
1 tablespoon light soy sauce
2 tablespoons A1 or Barbecue sauce
1 tablespoon Worcester sauce
1 tablespoon dry sherry
½ teaspoon sugar
pinch each of salt and white pepper
3 slices fresh ginger
2 cloves garlic
Sauce:
¼ cup water
¾ teaspoon chicken stock powder
1 teaspoon cornflour

Preparation:
Slice well-chilled pork thinly across the grain. Place in a bowl and add the seasoning ingredients with minced ginger and garlic. Mix well and leave for 2 hours, turning from time to time.
During last half hour sprinkle on 1 tablespoon oil and mix in.

Cooking:
Heat remaining oil in a heavy frying pan or wok and fry steaks for 1½ minutes on each side. Add sauce and bring to the boil. Simmer until the sauce thickens and becomes clear. Stir in plum sauce or jam and mix well.

Serving:
Garnish with finely chopped shallot or fresh coriander.

Shredded Pork with Beanshoots

375 g (¾ lb) lean pork, boneless
2 tablespoons pork marinade
2 egg whites
1 tablespoon cornflour
1½ tablespoons oil
250 g (½ lb) fresh beanshoots
3 shallots (or 1 medium onion)
½ red or green pepper
2 cloves garlic
4 tablespoons vegetable oil
Sauce:
¼ cup water
1 tablespoon chicken stock powder
2 teaspoons light soy sauce
½ teaspoon sugar
1 teaspoon sesame oil
¾ teaspoon cornflour

Preparation:
Slice well-chilled pork thinly across the grain, then cut into very fine shreds. Place in a bowl with marinade, egg whites, cornflour and oil. Mix well and leave for 20-25 minutes.
Rinse beanshoots in cold water and drain well. Remove roots and pods, if preferred. Shred shallots or thinly slice onion. Cut pepper into long shreds. Mince garlic. Mix sauce ingredients in a bowl.

Cooking:
Heat oil in a wok and fry garlic for a few seconds. Add shredded pork and stir-fry on high heat until it whitens, about 1½ minutes. Add onion and pepper and stir fry for 1½ minutes on high heat. Remove and keep warm.
Stir-fry beanshoots for 1½-2 minutes, then return the pork, mix well and pour in the sauce. Stir until it thickens and clears.

Serving:
Garnish with sprigs of parsley and pineapple chunks.

Braised Cantonese Beef

500 g (1 lb) fillet steak
3 tablespoons meat marinade
2 teaspoons cornflour
2 shallots
3 slices fresh ginger
3 cloves garlic
4 tablespoons vegetable oil
Sauce:
⅓ cup beef stock or consomme
2 teaspoons dark soy sauce
2 teaspoons light soy sauce
2 teaspoons Worcester sauce
1 tablespoon sweet barbecue sauce
1 tablespoon tomato sauce
2 teaspoons dry sherry
1 tablespoon sugar
1 teaspoon cornflour
pinch each salt and white pepper

Preparation:
Slice well-chilled meat into 1cm (¼″) steaks, across the grain. Place in a bowl and season with marinade and cornflour. Leave for 1 hour.
Shred shallot and ginger. Slice garlic. Mix sauce ingredients in a bowl.

Cooking:
Heat oil in a heavy frying pan or wok and fry garlic for 1 minute, then set aside, or discard. Add drained steaks and fry on high heat until lightly coloured. Turn and fry other side until coloured, about ¾ minute on each side. Add shredded shallot, sauce and reserved marinade and bring almost to the boil. Simmer until steaks are tender and sauce thickened.

Serving:
Arrange the steaks on a serving plate and garnish with reserved garlic or shredded shallot. Sprinkle on sesame oil and add a dusting of white pepper.

Shredded Beef with Green Vegetables

375 g (¾ lb) fillet or frying steak
2 tablespoons meat marinade
1 egg white
1 tablespoon cornflour
500 g (1 lb) Chinese cabbage or choy sum
2 teaspoons dry sherry
1 teaspoon sugar
½ teaspoon sesame oil
pinch of salt
4 tablespoons vegetable oil

Preparation:
Slice well-chilled beef thinly across the grain, then cut into fine shreds. Place in a bowl with marinade, egg white and cornflour. Mix well and leave for 40 minutes. Wash vegetables and cut into 10cm (4″) pieces. Hard stems should be diagonally sliced.

Cooking:
Bring a large pot of water to the boil and drop in vegetable stems. Boil for 1 minute, then drain and splash with cold water. Drain again.
Heat oil in a large wok and stir-fry drained beef until lightly coloured, about 2 minutes. Remove and set aside. Add leaves and stems of vegetables and sprinkle with sherry, sugar, sesame oil and salt. Stir-fry on high heat until just cooked through, but still crisp, about 2 minutes. Return meat and any remaining marinade and stir-fry briefly.

Serving:
Garnish with tomato wedges or slivers of red chilli. Season with a little sesame oil.

Beef with Chinese Pickles and Pineapple, page 26 ▶

Beef with Chinese Pickles and Pineapple

375 g (¾ lb) fillet or frying steak
2 tablespoons meat marinade
2 teaspoons cornflour
2 shallots
8 slices fresh young ginger
½ fresh red chilli
30 g (1 oz) preserved Chow Chow or Chinese
  pickles
90 g (3 oz) canned pineapple chunks,
  drained
3 tablespoons vegetable oil
Sauce:
4 tablespoons beef stock
3 tablespoons pineapple juice
1 teaspoon cornflour

Preparation:
Slice well-chilled beef thinly across the
grain, then cut into 2cm (¾") strips. Place in
a bowl, add marinade and cornflour, mix
well and leave for 45 minutes.
Cut shallots into 2.5cm (1") pieces. Shred
chilli and Chow Chow or pickles. Mix sauce
ingredients in a bowl.

Cooking:
Heat oil in a wok and fry drained beef until
the colour changes, about 2 minutes. Add
shallot, ginger and chilli and stir-fry for ½
minute more. Add sauce and reserved
marinade and stir-fry until the sauce
thickens. Check seasonings.
Add shredded Chow Chow or pickles and
pineapple chunks and heat through.

Serving:
Surround with wedges of pineapple and
sprigs of fresh parsley or coriander.

Vegetable Combination

250 g (½ lb) fresh Chinese green vegetables
90 g (30 oz) snow peas, long beans or frozen
  peas
90 g (3 oz) canned bamboo shoots, drained
6 spears canned asparagus, drained
6 canned water chestnuts, drained
4 dried black mushrooms, soaked
1 small onion
6 slices carrot
4 slices fresh ginger
3 tablespoons vegetable oil
Sauce:
¼ cup water
1 teaspoon chicken stock powder
1 tablespoon light soy sauce
1 teaspoon dry sherry
½ teaspoon sugar
½ teaspoon sesame oil (optional)
½ teaspoon cornflour
pinch each of salt and white pepper

Preparation:
Wash green vegetables and separate leaves
from hard stems. Slice stems diagonally.
Wash and string snow peas or beans. Cut
beans, if used, into 5cm (2") pieces.
Thinly slice bamboo shoots, cut asparagus
in halves and slice water chestnuts
horizontally. Drain and quarter
mushrooms. Slice onion.
Mix sauce ingredients in a bowl.

Cooking
Bring a saucepan of water to the boil and
boil vegetable stems for 1 minute, then add
carrot and boil for ½ minute. Drain. Boil
snow peas for a few seconds, or beans for 1
minute. If using peas, pour boiling water
over them to thaw.
Heat oil in a wok and stir-fry ginger and
onion for ½ minute. Add all vegetables and
stir-fry on moderately high heat for 2½-3
minutes until beginning to soften. Add sauce
and simmer, covered, until vegetables are
tender. Stir occasionally.

Serving:
Serve in a vegetable dish. Season with
sesame oil and white pepper.

Stir-Fried Mixed Vegetables

2 stalks celery
1 large red pepper
1 large onion
90 g (3 oz) canned button mushrooms,
  drained
125 g (¼ lb) canned baby corn cobs, drained
60 g (2 oz) raw baby shrimps, peeled
4 slices fresh ginger
90 g (3 oz) chicken breast
2 teaspoons poultry marinade
1 teaspoon cornflour
4 tablespoons vegetable oil
Sauce:
¼ cup water
1 teaspoon chicken stock powder
1 tablespoon light soy sauce
2 teaspoons dry sherry
½ teaspoon sugar
½ teaspoon sesame oil (optional)

Preparation:
Wipe celery and cut into 2.5cm (1") diagonal
slices. Cut pepper and onion into 2.5cm (1")
squares. Halve baby corn. Thoroughly wash
baby shrimp and drain well. Cut chicken
into 2.5cm (1") cubes and season with
marinade and cornflour. Leave for 10
minutes.
Mix sauce ingredients in a bowl.

Cooking:
Heat 1 tablespoon oil in a wok and stir-fry
celery for 1 minute, the add 2 tablespoons
water, cover and simmer for 1 more minute,
then remove lid and cook until the liquid
evaporates.
Add remaining oil with red pepper, onion,
mushrooms, corn and ginger and stir-fry for
2 minutes, then push to the side of the wok.
Add chicken and stir-fry for 1 minute, then
add the shrimps and stir-fry with chicken
until both are cooked through, about 1½
more minutes. Mix with the vegetables.
Pour in the sauce and stir-fry until the sauce
boils and begins to thicken and become
clear.

Serving:
Transfer to a serving plate and sprinkle on a
little more sesame oil before serving.

Crabmeat Omelette, page 28 ▶

Beanshoot Salad

625 g (1¼ lb) fresh beanshoots
1 small red pepper
½ fresh red chilli
1-2 cloves garlic
1 teaspoon coarsely ground black pepper
1 tablespoon lemon juice
1 teaspoon salt
1 teaspoon sugar
2-3 tablespoons vegetable oil

Preparation:
Rinse beanshoots in cold water. Drain well. Remove roots and pods. Dry on kitchen paper.
Cut pepper and chilli into long shreds.

Cooking:
Heat oil in a wok and stir-fry minced garlic and black pepper for ½ minute on moderate heat. Add beanshoots with pepper and chilli and stir-fry until the beanshoots begin to soften and turn transparent, about 2½ minutes.
Remove from the heat. Add lemon juice, salt and sugar and mix well. Leave to cool.

Serving:
Pile into a dish or salad bowl and surround with tomato wedges.

Crabmeat Omelette

6 eggs
1½ tablespoons water
½ teaspoon salt
1 tablespoon cornflour
1 tablespoon vegetable oil
200 g (7 oz) fresh, frozen or canned crab meat
2 tablespoons vegetable oil
Seasonings:
1 tablespoon light soy sauce
1 teaspoon dry sherry
½ teaspoon sesame oil
pinch of white pepper

Preparation:
Lightly beat eggs and add water, salt, cornflour and 1 tablespoon oil. Beat until smooth.

Cooking
Place frozen crabmeat, if used, in a wok and add seasonings and oil. Cover and simmer on low heat until thawed. Raise heat, remove lid and cook until liquid has evaporated.
If using fresh or canned crab meat, cook with the seasoning ingredients and oil in a wok for 1-1½ minutes. Stir to break up any lumps.
Pour in egg mixture, mix with the crab and re-cover. Cook on low heat until the omelette is firm enough to turn. Cut in halves, turn over and raise heat to brown underside.

Serving:
Place the two halves overlapped on a serving plate and garnish with fresh coriander and thin slices of red chilli.

Fried Rice ▶

750 g (1½ lb) cooked white rice
125 g (¼ lb) frozen green peas
5 dried black mushrooms, soaked
125 g (¼ lb) Chinese roast pork or raw baby shrimps, peeled
2 shallots (or 1 small onion)
2 eggs
1 tablespoon light soy sauce
30 g (1 oz) pineapple chunks (optional)
4 tablespoons vegetable oil
pinch each of salt and white pepper

Preparation:
Spread rice on a tray and break up any lumps. Leave to dry out slightly before using.
Pour boiling water over peas to thaw. Drain well. Squeeze water from mushrooms, remove stems and slice thinly. Cut roast pork into small dice. Thaw shrimps, if frozen. Chop shallots or onion and lightly beat eggs.

Cooking:
Wipe out a wok with an oiled cloth, heat well, then pour in the beaten egg. Turn pan quickly to spread egg into a very thin omelette. Cook until firm, then flip over and cook other side briefly. Lift out and leave to cool.
Pour 1 tablespoon oil into the pan and fry shallots or onion with peas for 1 minute. Remove. Add more oil and fry pork or shrimps for 1-1¼ minutes, then add mushrooms and stir-fry for a few seconds more. Add soy sauce and stir until well mixed, then remove from the pan.
Heat remaining oil and stir-fry rice on moderately high heat until each grain is coated with the oil. Add salt and white pepper.
Roll up the egg and cut into fine shreds. Add half to the rice with pork or shrimps and vegetables. Mix thoroughly and heat through.

Serving:
Stir in pineapple chunks, if used, and garnish with fresh coriander or thinly sliced red chilli and remaining shredded omelette.

Chicken Chow Mein

4-5 bundles (about 185 g/6 oz) thin egg
  noodles
250 g (½ lb) chicken breast
1 tablespoon poultry marinade
2 teaspoons cornflour
125 g (¼ lb) fresh beanshoots
2 shallots (or 1 small onion)
4 canned water chestnuts, drained
60 g (2 oz) canned bamboo shoots, drained
2 stalks celery
1 slice fresh ham
2 eggs
vegetable oil
Sauce:
⅓ cup water
1 teaspoon chicken stock powder
1 tablespoon light soy sauce
1 teaspoon cornflour
pinch each salt and white pepper

Preparation:
Soak noodles in hot water for 10 minutes to
soften. Pull bundles apart, drain well and
spread on a tray to partially dry.
Shred chilled chicken and season with
marinade and cornflour. Leave for 10
minutes.
Rinse beanshoots in cold water and drain
well. Remove roots and pods, if preferred.
Shred shallots or thinly slice onion. Slice
water chestnuts horizontally and slice
bamboo shoots and celery. Shred ham and
lightly beat eggs.
Mix sauce ingredients in a bowl.

Cooking:
Wipe out a wok with a well oiled cloth, heat
well, then pour in the egg. Turn the pan
quickly to make a thin omelette and cook on
moderate heat on both sides. Remove and
leave to cool.
Pour in 3 tablespoons oil and fry noodles on
high heat on both sides until edges are crisp.
Lift onto a serving plate and keep warm.
Add another 1½ tablespoons oil and stir-fry
chicken with shallots or onion on high heat
for 1 minute. Remove. Add celery, bamboo
shoots and water chestnuts and stir-fry for 2
minutes, adding a little more oil if needed.
Add beanshoots and stir-fry for 1-1½
minutes.
Return chicken and mix all together well,
then pour in the sauce and bring to the boil.
Simmer until thickened. Spoon chicken and
vegetables over the noodles. Arrange
shredded ham on top. Finely shred the
omelette and use to garnish the edges of the
plate. Add a few sprigs of fresh parsley or
coriander.

Soft-Fried Noodles with Beef and Vegetables ▶

4 bundles (about 150 g/5 oz) thin egg
noodles
250 g (½ lb) frying steak
3 tablespoons meat marinade
2 teaspoons cornflour
90 g (3 oz) fresh beanshoots
60 g (2 oz) long or green beans
1 small carrot
1 stalk celery
1 small onion
3 slices fresh ginger
5 tablespoons vegetable oil
Sauce:
½ cup beef stock or consomme
1 tablespoon dark soy sauce
2 teaspoons dry sherry
½ teaspoon sugar
1 teaspoon sesame oil
1½ teaspoons cornflour
pinch each of salt and white pepper

Preparation:
Drop noodles into boiling water to soften.
Leave until bundles can be pulled apart,
about 10 minutes. Drain well. Slice well-
chilled beef thinly across the grain, then cut
into fine shreds. Place in a bowl with
marinade and cornflour, mix well and leave
for 45 minutes.
Rinse beanshoots in cold water, remove
pods and roots, if preferred. Slice beans into
5cm (2″) lengths and cut carrot and celery
into matchstick pieces of the same length.
Thinly slice onion. Shred ginger.
Mix sauce ingredients in a bowl.

Cooking:
Heat 2 tablespoons oil in a wok and fry
noodles until slightly crisped on the
underside. Cut into four sections and turn to
fry other side, adding an additional 1
tablespoon of oil. When crisped, lift onto a
serving plate and keep warm. Add
remaining oil, heat the wok to very hot and
stir-fry drained beef with ginger for 1¼-2
minutes. Remove.
Add vegetables and stir-fry for ½ minute,
then pour in the sauce and any remaining
marinade and bring to the boil. Reduce heat
and simmer, covered, until vegetables have
softened, but retain some crispness. Return
meat and heat through.

Serving:
Pour meat and vegetables with the sauce
over the noodles, and garnish the plate with
wedges of tomato.

Roast Pork with Soup Noodles

4 bundles (about 150 g/5 oz) thin egg
noodles
250 g (½ lb) Chinese roast pork
8-10 leaves green vegetable (spinach, lettuce
or cabbage)
1 shallot
3 slices fresh ginger
5 cups water
1 tablespoon chicken stock powder
2 teaspoons light soy sauce
1 tablespoon vegetable oil
½ teaspoon sesame oil
salt and white pepper to taste

Preparation:
Soak noodles in warm water for 10 minutes
to soften. Pull bundles apart and drain well.
Thinly slice pork, then cut into narrow
strips. Chop shallot, shred ginger, wash
vegetables and drain.

Cooking:
Place sliced pork in a pot. Add shallot,
ginger, water and stock powder and bring to
the boil.
Season with soy sauce, sesame oil and oil.
Reduce heat and simmer for 20 minutes,
then add noodles and cook until tender. Add
salt and pepper to taste.
Add vegetables and simmer gently for 1
minute.

Serving:
Pour into a casserole or soup tureen and
garnish with sprigs of coriander or parsley.
Sprinkle on extra white pepper and sesame
oil before serving.

From the North

Led by the renowned Peking Duck, dishes that originated in the North reflect the magnificence of old Imperial China. Dishes, such as Jade Prawns and Asparagus Fish Rolls epitomise two key elements of Northern cooking — understatement of seasoning and perfection in cooking. The flavours stand out, but do not overpower the main ingredients. The food is tasty and nourishing, but is less rich and heavy than its neighbouring cuisines to the East and West.

Where rice is the staple in the South, Northern menus include rice as a main dish, in the form of exotic flavoured dishes, and rely on wheat flour breads, buns and pancakes to add bulk to a meal. Frequently meats, and even vegetables, are designed to be wrapped in thin griddle-cooked pancakes, as in the case of Peking Duck and Deep-fried Spiced Duck, or used as a stuffing for hollow pan-fried crisp buns. Sweet bean sauces and onion or cucumber being added for extra flavour.

Vegetables are often given especially interesting treatment, exemplified by the Fried Bamboo Shoots with Dried Scallops which are deep-fried and flavoured with crisp-fried dried seafood and preserved or other green vegetables.

Meat dishes, that carry a hint of the lusty Mongolian influence, are predominant in this cuisine. Even lamb and mutton, rarely eaten in other parts of China, are popular here and are served roasted, braised, stewed, stir-fried or cooked in two exciting fashions adopted centuries ago from the Mongol chefs — barbecues and hotpots of thinly shaved slices of the meat, cooked quickly with a variety of vegetables.

Asparagus Fish Rolls ▶

625 g (1¼ lb) fillets of flounder, whiting or bream
½ teaspoon salt
pinch of white pepper
12 spears canned asparagus, drained
½ cup cornflour
2 egg whites
2-2½ cups dry white breadcrumbs
deep-frying oil

Preparation:
Cut fillets into 12 pieces, each about 12cm × 4cm (5" × 1½"). Season with salt and white pepper. Cut asparagus in halves.
Wrap each strip of fish around two pieces of asparagus and secure with toothpicks. Coat thickly with cornflour and leave for about 5 minutes.
Lightly beat egg whites and brush over the fish rolls, then coat generously with breadcrumbs.

Cooking:
Heat deep oil to hot in a wok or saucepan. Reduce heat slightly and put in fish rolls, several at a time to keep the oil hot. Deep-fry for about 1½ minutes, then lift out and drain.
Before serving, reheat the oil and briefly re-fry the fish rolls until the surface is crisp and golden.

Serving:
Place on paper napkins and surround with sliced cucumber. Serve with small dishes of light soy sauce and spicy salt.

Crispy Whole Fish Sweet and Sour ▶

750 g (1½ lb) flathead, mullet or bream
2 tablespoons seafood marinade
1 cup cornflour
2 egg whites
deep-frying oil
Sauce:
½ green pepper
1 small carrot
4 slices fresh ginger
½ fresh red chilli
1 shallot
1-2 cloves garlic
2 tablespoons frozen green peas
¾ cup water
1 teaspoon chicken stock powder
1 tablespoon light soy sauce
1½ tablespoons tomato sauce
½ cup white vinegar
125 g (¼ lb) sugar
1 tablespoon vegetable oil
2 teaspoons cornflour
½ teaspoon salt
pinch of white pepper

Preparation:
Clean fish and score in a criss-cross fashion across the body on each side. Season with marinade and leave for 10 minutes, then thickly coat with cornflour and leave for 10 more minutes.
Prepare the sauce by cutting all vegetables into fine dice. Drop carrots and peas into boiling water and cook for 1-2 minutes, then drain. Mix remaining ingredients in a small saucepan.
Lightly beat egg whites and brush over the fish. Coat thickly with remaining cornflour.

Cooking:
Heat deep oil in a pan large enough to hold the fish flat. When very hot, put in the fish (it should be covered with the oil) and reduce heat slightly. Deep-fry, turning once, for about 8 minutes.
When ready, the fish should be well-crisped and a light golden colour. Lift out carefully and drain well. Set on a large oval serving plate and keep warm.
Bring sauce to the boil. Add the prepared vegetables and simmer for 5 minutes. Pour into a sauceboat or jug.

Serving:
Garnish the fish with carrot and cucumber slices and sprigs of parsley. Serve the sauce separately to pour over the fish at the table.

Pineapple Fish

750 g (1½ lb) fillets of bream or flounder
3 tablespoons seafood marinade
2 egg whites
4 tablespoons cornflour
6 slices fresh ginger
1 small green pepper
4 slices canned pineapple, drained
1 tablespoon preserved Chow Chow or
    Chinese pickles
deep-frying oil
Sauce:
⅓ cup water
1 teaspoon chicken stock powder
¼ cup pineapple juice
½ teaspoon white vinegar
2 teaspoons sugar
2 teaspoons cornflour
pinch each of salt and white pepper

Preparation:
Cut fish fillets into bite-sized pieces and season with marinade. Leave for 10 minutes. Coat with lightly beaten egg white, then place in a plastic bag with cornflour. Shake the bag vigorously to thickly coat the fish with flour.
Shred ginger and cut pepper into long shreds. Chop pineapple and Chow Chow or pickles.
Mix sauce ingredients in a bowl.

Cooking:
Heat deep oil in a wok and when moderately hot add the fish pieces, several at a time, after shaking off excess flour. Deep-fry until cooked through and lightly coloured, about 3 minutes. Lift out and drain well.
In a clean wok heat 1 tablespoon of the oil and add the sauce. Bring to the boil, then add ginger, pepper, pineapple and pickles. Simmer for 3 minutes. Return fish and heat through.

Serving:
Arrange fish and vegetables on a serving plate and pour on the sauce. Garnish with sprigs of parsley and thinly sliced lemon.

Seafood Combination

185 g (6 oz) fish fillets
186 g (6 oz) raw prawns, peeled
125 g (¼ lb) fresh squid, cleaned
90 g (3 oz) canned abalone, drained
125 g (¼ lb) raw baby shrimps, peeled
3 tablespoons seafood marinade
1 tablespoon cornflour
60 g (2 oz) canned bamboo shoots, drained
60 g (2 oz) frozen green peas
1 small carrot
1 medium onion
2 slices fresh ginger
6 pigeon's eggs (optional)
4-5 tablespoons vegetable oil
Sauce:
¾ cup water
1½ teaspoons chicken stock powder
1 tablespoon light soy sauce
2 teaspoons dry sherry
1½ teaspoons cornflour
pinch each of salt and white pepper

Preparation:
Slice well-chilled fish into thin, bite-sized pieces. Rinse prawns and cut large ones in halves. Cut squid into 2.5cm (1") squares. Rinse baby shrimps and drain well. Place the seafood in a bowl and season with marinade and cornflour. Mix well and leave for 10 minutes.
Thinly slice bamboo shoots. Plunge peas into boiling water to thaw. Slice carrot and onion. Shred ginger.
Hard-boil eggs, if used. Cover with cold water.
Mix sauce ingredients in a bowl.

Cooking:
Drop carrots into a pot of boiling water to cook for 45 seconds. Drain, then blanch onion for 20 seconds. Drain.
Heat half the oil in a wok and when very hot, stir-fry bamboo shoots, carrot and onion for 1½ minutes.
Add peas and stir-fry for a few seconds more, then remove. Pour in remaining oil and stir-fry seafood with ginger for 2-2½ minutes on moderately high heat.
Return vegetables, pour in the sauce and bring to the boil. Simmer, stirring, until sauce thickens slightly. Add shelled eggs and heat through.

Serving:
Transfer to a serving plate and surround with lemon and cucumber slices. Serve with soy sauce.

Crab in Black Bean Sauce ▶

3 small (or 1 large) mud crabs
1 tablespoon salted black beans
3 cloves garlic
1½ teaspoons sugar
1 tablespoon light soy sauce
2 teaspoons dry sherry
1 tablespoon vegetable oil
3 slices fresh ginger
2 shallots (or 1 small onion)
1-2 cloves garlic (optional)
3 tablespoons vegetable oil
Sauce:
¾ cup water
1¼ teaspoons chicken stock powder
2 teaspoons cornflour

Preparation:
Clean crabs with a brush and wash well. Break away undershells and remove mouth, stomach and spongy "fingers." Chop bodies into quarters, legs attached. Break off claws and crack shells to allow sauce to penetrate. Crush black beans with garlic and sugar, then mix with soy sauce, sherry and 1 tablespoon vegetable oil. Shred ginger, chop shallots or onion and mince garlic, if used. Mix sauce ingredients in a bowl.

Cooking:
Heat oil in a wok and stir-fry shallot or onion with garlic, if used, for 1 minute. Remove and set aside. Add crabs and ginger and stir-fry on moderately high heat until they change colour, about 5 minutes. Add the black bean paste and stir-fry for a few more minutes, returning onion and garlic to the pan.
Pour in the sauce and stir until boiling. Reduce heat and simmer until crabs are cooked through, about 2 more minutes.

Serving:
Arrange the crab pieces on a plate and garnish with parsley and chopped red chilli.

Note:
Add chopped red chilli to the sauce in last few minutes of cooking, for extra flavour and a slight hotness.

Black Bean Lobster and Prawn Balls

375 g (¾ lb) large raw prawns, peeled
375 g (¾ lb) lobster meat
1 small green pepper
2 shallots (or 1 small onion)
1 fresh red chilli
6 slices fresh ginger
2-3 cloves garlic
2 tablespoons salted black beans
2 teaspoons sugar
deep-frying oil
Sauce:
½ cup water
½ teaspoon chicken stock powder
1 teaspoon cornflour
pinch each of sugar and white pepper

Preparation:
Cut prawns and lobster into 2.5cm (1")
cubes.
Cut peppers and shallots or onion into thin
shreds. Shred chilli, ginger and garlic. Crush
black beans with sugar. Mix sauce
ingredients in a bowl.

Cooking:
Heat deep oil to hot in a wok and reduce
heat slightly. Deep-fry lobster and prawns
until pink, about ¾ minute. Remove and
drain well.
Pour off all but 2-2½ tablespoons oil and
stir-fry garlic lightly. Add ginger, shallots or
onion and green pepper and stir-fry for 1
minute on high heat.
Add bean paste and chilli and stir-fry for 1
more minute, after reducing heat slightly.
Return prawns and lobster and stir briefly to
mix with the vegetables.
Pour in the sauce, bring to the boil, and stir
until the sauce thickens and clears.

Serving:
Garnish with chopped fresh coriander or
shallots.

Deep-Fried Garlic Prawns

500 g (1 lb) medium raw prawns, peeled
1 tablespoon seafood marinade
3 egg whites
3 tablespoons cornflour
1½ tablespoons plain flour
⅓ teaspoon bicarbonate of soda
¼ teaspoon salt
1 fresh red chilli
3 cloves garlic
1-2 shallots
1 tablespoon dry sherry
1 tablespoon sesame oil
deep-frying oil
Sauce:
¼ cup water
¾ teaspoon chicken stock powder
¾ teaspoon cornflour
pinch each sugar, salt and white pepper
pinch chilli powder (optional)

Preparation:
Slit prawns down centre backs and remove
dark veins. Cut each prawn in halves, across
the body and rinse in cold water. Pat dry
with kitchen paper. Season with marinade
and leave for 5 minutes.
Mix lightly beaten egg whites with
cornflour, plain flour, bicarbonate of soda
and salt, adding just enough water to make a
thickish batter. Beat well.
Finely chop chilli and garlic. Cut shallots
into 2.5cm (1") pieces.
Mix sauce ingredients in a bowl.

Cooking:
Heat deep oil in a wok or sauce pan to very
hot and add sesame oil. Reduce heat
slightly. Dip prawns into the batter and
drop into the oil several at a time to keep the
oil hot. Deep-fry prawns to a golden colour,
about 1½ minutes. Lift out and drain.
Pour off all but 1 tablespoon oil and fry
shallot, garlic and chilli lightly. Add the
prawns and pour in the sherry. Stir-fry
briefly on high heat, then pour in the sauce.
Bring to the boil and cook, stirring, on high
heat until the sauce becomes clear.

Serving:
Garnish with fresh coriander and cubes of
pineapple.

"Jade Prawns"

750 g (1½ lb) large raw prawns, in shells
2 tablespoons seafood marinade
1 tablespoon cornflour
250 g (½ lb) fresh broccoli
1 tablespoon dry sherry
3 slices fresh ginger
pinch each of sugar, salt and bicarbonate of
   soda
½ teaspoon sesame oil
deep-frying oil
Sauce:
¼ cup water
½ teaspoon chicken stock powder
1 teaspoon dry sherry
½ teaspoon salt
½ teaspoon sugar
½ teaspoon sesame oil
½ teaspoon cornflour

Preparation:
Remove heads and shells from prawns,
leaving tails on. Slit down centre backs and
remove dark veins. Rinse well and pat dry
with kitchen paper. Season with marinade
and cornflour and leave for 10 minutes.
Divide broccoli into florets and rinse well.
Drain. Mix sauce ingredients in a bowl.

Cooking:
Bring enough water to cover the broccoli to
the boil and add sherry, ginger, sugar, salt
and bicarbonate of soda.
Add broccoli florets and boil for 2-2½
minutes, then drain and splash with cold
water to brighten colour. Drain and set
aside.
Heat deep oil to very hot in a wok or
saucepan and then reduce heat slightly. Add
prawns and cook for 1½ minutes. Remove
and drain.
Pour off all but 1 tablespoon oil and add the
sauce. Bring to the boil and when beginning
to thicken return prawns and broccoli and
heat through.
Season with sesame oil.

Serving:
Arrange the broccoli around the edge of a
serving plate and pile prawns in the centre.
Garnish with chopped red chilli.

Butterfly Prawn Cutlets

12 large raw prawns, in shells
2 teaspoons seafood marinade
2 tablespoons cornflour
2 egg whites
1¼-1½ cups dry white breadcrumbs
deep-frying oil

Preparation:
Remove heads and shells from prawns, but leave tails on. Slit down centre backs, cutting almost through. Remove dark veins. Rinse with cold water, pat dry with kitchen paper, then press each cutlet flat.
Season with marinade and leave for 5 minutes.
Coat lightly with cornflour and leave 5 more minutes. Beat egg whites.

Cooking:
Heat deep oil to very hot in a wok or saucepan. Reduce heat slightly. Dip prawns into beaten egg whites, then coat thickly with breadcrumbs.
Deep-fry, several at a time, in the hot oil until golden, about 2 minutes. Remove and drain well.

Serving:
Line a serving plate with paper napkins and place prawns on top. Add parsley and lemon wedges. Serve with dips of soy sauce or spicy tomato sauce.

Lemon Chicken ▶

1½ kg (3 lb) spring chicken
2 tablespoons poultry marinade
½ cup cornflour
½ cup plain flour
2 eggs
¾ teaspoon salt
1 teaspoon bicarbonate of soda
yellow food colouring (optional)
deep-frying oil
Sauce:
¾ cup water
1¼ teaspoons chicken stock powder
⅓ cup lemon juice
1 tablespoon vegetable oil
1¾ teaspoons white vinegar
90 g (3 oz) sugar
1 teaspoon sesame oil (optional)
1 tablespoon cornflour
yellow food colouring (optional)

Preparation:
Clean chicken, wash and pat dry. Cut in halves down the back, and through the breast bone. Rub the two halves with marinade and leave for 15 minutes. If preferred, the chicken can be chopped into bite-sized pieces.
Mix cornflour, flour, beaten eggs, salt and bicarbonate of soda, adding enough cold water to make a batter of coating consistency (thick enough not to run immediately off the back of a spoon).
Colour a light yellow, if desired.
Mix sauce ingredients in a small saucepan, adding just enough yellow food colouring, if used, to make a light yellow colour.

Cooking:
Bring sauce to the boil, stirring constantly, and simmer until slightly thickened and beginning to clear, about 5 minutes. Remove from the heat.
Heat deep oil to very hot in a large wok, then reduce heat slightly. Coat the chicken, or chicken pieces, thickly with the batter and deep-fry half at a time, until the surface is crisp and golden and meat cooked through, about 7 minutes for halved chicken, 3 minutes for chicken pieces. Lift out and drain well. Cook remaining chicken.
Cut halved chicken into serving pieces.

Serving:
Arrange chicken on a plate and garnish with thinly sliced lemon. Reheat the sauce and pour over the chicken just before serving, or take separately to the table.

Black Bean Chicken

625 g (1¼ lb) chicken pieces
1 set chicken giblets (optional)
2½ tablespoons poultry marinade
1 tablespoon cornflour
2 tablespoons salted black beans
1½ tablespoons dry sherry
2-3 teaspoons sugar
2-3 cloves garlic
2 shallots (or 1 small onion)
1 tablespoon light soy sauce
½ teaspoon dark soy sauce
deep-frying oil

Preparation:
Skin and bone chicken, if preferred, and cut into bite-sized pieces. Wash and slice giblets, if used. Season chicken and giblets with marinade and cornflour and leave for 20 minutes.
Crush black beans with sherry, sugar and garlic.
Slice shallots or onion.

Cooking:
Heat deep oil to moderately hot in a wok or large saucepan and deep-fry chicken and giblets until lightly coloured and half cooked, about 3 minutes. Lift out and drain well. Pour off all but 3 tablespoons oil and fry shallots with black bean paste for 1 minute. Return chicken, add soy sauces and stir-fry on high heat until chicken is cooked through, about 1 minute.

Serving:
Arrange on a plate and decorate with tomato slices and fresh coriander or parsley.

Soy Sauce Chicken

1½ kg (3 lb) chicken
10 slices fresh ginger
4 shallots (or 1 medium onion)
4 points star anise
1 small piece cinnamon bark (optional)
1 teaspoon sesame oil
Sauce:
1½ cups water
½ teaspoon chicken stock powder
1 cup light soy sauce
½ cup dark soy sauce
2 tablespoons dry sherry
75 g (2½ oz) sugar
2.5cm (1") piece fresh ginger, peeled

Preparation:
Clean chicken, wash and pat dry. Place sliced ginger and shallots or coarsely chopped onion in the cavity and put chicken into a large saucepan. Add star anise and cinnamon. Mix sauce ingredients in a small saucepan and bring to the boil. Pour over the chicken, add enough boiling water to just cover the bird.

Cooking:
Cover the saucepan and bring just to the boil, then reduce heat to very low and simmer chicken, turning once or twice, for about 45 minutes. Lift out and drain well. Rub with sesame oil, then cut into bite-sized pieces.

Serving:
Arrange on a plate and garnish with sliced tomato and cucumber. Serve hot or cool.

Note:
As an alternative, drain the chicken well, then deep-fry in plenty of oil until dark and crisp on the surface. Slice thinly and serve with Mandarin Pancakes, sliced shallots and cucumber and Hoisin or Plum sauce.

Mandarin Pancakes

(Makes 12)
2½ cups plain flour
¾ cup boiling water
¼ cup cold water
1 tablespoon vegetable or sesame oil

Preparation:
Sift flour into a mixing bowl and make a well in the centre. Pour in boiling water and mix loosely, then add cold water and work with a wooden spoon until cool enough to knead.
Knead until dough is smooth and pliable, about 6 minutes. Leave, covered with a damp cloth, until needed.
Roll into a sausage shape and cut into 12 pieces.
Roll each out to about 1cm (¼") thick and brush one side only with vegetable or sesame oil.
Place two pancakes together, oiled sides inwards. Roll out as thinly as possible.

Cooking:
Heat a heavy iron frying pan or hot plate and wipe with a well-oiled cloth. Cook the pancakes one at a time on moderate to low heat until lightly speckled underneath. Turn and cook other side.
The pancakes should not be allowed to become crisp. Remove from the pan and carefully pull the two pancakes apart. Fold into triangles and cover with a warm cloth until needed.

Deep-Fried Spiced Duck

3 kg (6 lb) duck
2 teaspoons five spices powder
1 teaspoon brown peppercorns (or ground black pepper)
2 teaspoons salt
1½ teaspoons sugar
3 tablespoons dry sherry
6 slices fresh ginger
2 whole star anise
2 tablespoons dark soy sauce
2 teaspoons sesame oil
deep-frying oil

Preparation:
Clean duck and wash well. Wipe dry inside and out.
Mix five spices powder with finely ground brown or black pepper, salt, sugar and sherry and rub over the duck and inside the cavity.
Place ginger and star anise in the cavity. Leave for 1 hour.

Cooking:
Place duck on a fireproof dish and steam over gently boiling water for 3 hours, or in a pressure cooker for ½ hour. Remove and leave to cool. Rub with soy sauce.
Heat enough oil to half cover duck in a large wok or saucepan, and when very hot reduce heat slightly and add sesame oil. Put in the duck and deep-fry on both sides for 4 minutes. Lift out and leave to cool for 15 minutes. Return and fry for 4 minutes more on each side and remove again.
Repeat this cooking process once or twice more until the duck is very crisp on the surface. The meat will be almost dry and crunchy. Drain well.

Serving:
Serve with spicy salt and Hoisin or Plum sauce, Mandarin Pancakes and sliced shallots. The meat can be stripped away from the bones in slivers, using chopsticks or a fork.

Pork in Barbecue Sauce

625 g (1¼ lb) pork fillet
½ teaspoon five spices powder
½ teaspoon salt
2 teaspoons sugar
1 clove garlic
2 shallots (or 1 small onion)
2 slices fresh ginger
½ fresh red chilli
½ green pepper
3 tablespoons vegetable oil
Sauce:
½ cup water
¾ teaspoon chicken or beef stock powder
2 tablespoons dark soy sauce
3 tablespoons Hoisin or barbecue sauce
1½ tablespoons sugar or honey
½ teaspoon cornflour

Preparation:
Slice well-chilled pork fillet across the grain into 1cm (¼") escalopes. Season with five spices powder, salt and sugar, rubbing in lightly. Leave for 30 minutes, then pound with the blunt edge of a cleaver to tenderise. Slice garlic and onions and shred ginger and chilli. Cut pepper into long shreds.
Mix sauce ingredients in a bowl.

Cooking:
Heat oil in a wok and fry pork on high heat until it begins to whiten. Turn once or twice only.
Push to one side of the pan. Add onion and garlic and stir-fry for ½ minute, then add ginger and pepper and stir-fry for 1 minute more.
Pour in the pre-mixed sauce and stir to thoroughly coat the pork escalopes.
Simmer until the sauce thickens and pork is tender, about 5 minutes on moderately low heat.

Serving:
Garnish with sliced cucumber and cubes of pineapple.

Sweet Pork with Green Vegetables ▶

1 kg (2 lb) pork shoulder or leg, boneless
1 dried red chilli
½ teaspoon brown peppercorns (or ground black pepper)
2 points star anise
6 cups cold water
500 g (1 lb) Chinese cabbage
Sauce:
¼ cup dark soy sauce
½ cup dry sherry
3 tablespoons brown sugar or honey
2 tablespoons oil
¼ teaspoon white pepper

Preparation:
Place the whole piece of pork in a saucepan and add chilli, peppercorns or pepper, star anise and water.
Wash cabbage and cut into 5cm (2") pieces.
Mix the sauce ingredients in a bowl.

Cooking:
Bring pork to boil, cover and simmer at low temperature for at least 1¼ hours.
Drain off half the water and discard spices. Add sauce and return to the boil. Reduce heat and simmer, covered, for about 2 hours, turning occasionally.
Lift out and drain well, then slice thinly.
Drop cabbage into the pan and simmer in the sauce for 2 minutes.

Serving:
Arrange cabbage in a deep serving bowl and place sliced pork on top. Pour on some of the reserved sauce and serve extra sauce separately with steamed white rice.

Stir-Fried Kidneys with Vegetables

375 g (¾ lb) pork kidneys
1½ stalks celery
1 medium carrot
30 g (1 oz) canned bamboo shoots, drained
2 shallots (or 1 small onion)
6 slices fresh ginger
3 cloves garlic
4 tablespoons vegetable oil
Sauce:
4 tablespoons water
¾ teaspoon chicken stock powder
2 teaspoons light soy sauce
1 teaspoon dry sherry
½ teaspoon white vinegar
½ teaspoon sugar
½ teaspoon cornflour
pinch each of salt and white pepper

Preparation:
Soak kidneys in cold water for 10 minutes, then cut into thin slices, removing any fat and membranes. Cut celery, carrot and bamboo shoots into matchstick pieces.
Drop carrot and celery into boiling water to blanch for ½ minute. Drain.
Slice shallots or onion, shred ginger and mince garlic.
Mix sauce ingredients in a bowl.

Cooking:
Bring a saucepan of water to the boil and drop in the sliced kidney. Return to the boil, then remove from the heat and leave for 2 minutes. Drain kidneys and leave to cool.
Heat oil in a wok and stir-fry kidneys until no pink shows. Push to one side of the pan and stir-fry shallots or onion, ginger and garlic for 1 minute. Add vegetables and stir-fry on moderately high heat for 2 minutes.
Mix all ingredients together, then pour in the sauce and bring to the boil. Stir until sauce thickens and becomes clear.

Serving:
Serve with a dip of white vinegar with shredded ginger and a little sugar added.

Seasoned Leg of Lamb ▶

2-2½ kg (4-5 lb) leg of lamb
5 slices fresh ginger
2 shallots (or 1 small onion)
2 tablespoons dark soy sauce
1 tablespoon dry sherry
1 whole star anise
1 small piece cinnamon bark
750 g (1½ lb) trimmed leeks
Sauce:
4 tablespoons water
4 tablespoons dark soy sauce
2 tablespoons sweet bean paste or Hoisin
   sauce
1½ tablespoons dry sherry
3 tablespoons sugar
2 teaspoons sesame oil

Preparation:
Place lamb leg in a large pot and add ginger, shallots, dark soy sauce, sherry and spices. Cover with cold water. Cut leeks into 2.5cm (1″) diagonal slices and rinse well in cold water. Drain.
Mix sauce ingredients in a small saucepan.

Cooking:
Bring lamb stock to boil over high heat, cover and reduce heat to moderately low. Simmer for 2 hours, or until meat is very tender. Lift out and drain well.
Boil leeks for 1 minute in salted water. Drain. Place lamb in a fireproof casserole and pour on the sauce. Cover and braise for about 15 minutes, turning once.
Add leeks and continue to cook on moderate heat until they are tender. Turn the meat from time to time and stir leeks. Add a little water or reserved stock if the sauce dries up.
Cut meat into paper thin slices and return to the sauce to reheat briefly.

Serving:
Arrange the sliced meat, overlapped, on a serving plate. Serve with Mandarin Pancakes, Hoisin or Plum sauce and the braised leeks.

Sliced Beef with Hot Peppers

500 g (1 lb) fillet or frying steak
3 tablespoons meat marinade
2 teaspoons cornflour
3 shallots (or 1 medium onion)
2 cloves garlic
3 dried red chillies
1 piece dried tangerine peel (or ½ orange
   peel)
3 tablespoons vegetable oil
Sauce:
3 tablespoons beef stock or consomme
2 tablespoons dark soy sauce
1 tablespoon dry sherry
1 teaspoon sugar
1 teaspoon sesame oil (optional)
½ teaspoon cornflour

Preparation:
Slice well-chilled beef very thinly across the grain, then cut into narrows strips. Season with marinade and cornflour and leave for 45 minutes. If using frying steak, pound with the blunt edge of a cleaver to tenderise.
Shred shallots or thinly slice onion. Chop garlic.
Mix sauce ingredients in a bowl.
Cut dried chillies and tangerine peel each into several pieces.

Cooking:
Heat oil in a wok and when very hot stir-fry dried chillies and tangerine peel until they darken. Remove and set aside. Add drained beef and garlic and stir-fry on high heat for 2 minutes. Remove meat, then stir-fry shallot or onion for 1½ minutes. Return meat and pour in the sauce. Bring to the boil, stirring until the sauce thickens and becomes clear. Return chilli and tangerine peel and heat through.

Serving:
Garnish with chopped parsley and red chilli.

Sliced Black Bean Beef

500 g (1 lb) fillet or frying steak
3 tablespoons meat marinade
2 teaspoons cornflour
1 green pepper
½ red pepper
1 medium onion
3 slices fresh ginger
2 tablespoons salted black beans
2 teaspoons sugar
4 cloves garlic
1 tablespoon dark soy sauce
1 tablespoon dry sherry
1 teaspoon sesame oil
pinch of white pepper
4-5 tablespoons vegetable oil
Sauce:
½ cup beef stock or consomme
1 teaspoon cornflour

Preparation:
Slice well-chilled beef very thinly across the grain.
Season with marinade and cornflour and leave for 45 minutes. If using frying steak, pound with the blunt edge of a cleaver to tenderise.
Cut green and red peppers and onion into 2cm (¾″) squares. Crush black beans with sugar and garlic. Mix with soy sauce, sherry, sesame oil and pepper.
Mix sauce ingredients in a small bowl.

Cooking:
Bring a pot of water to boil. Drop in peppers and onion to blanch for 20 seconds. Drain and splash with cold water. Drain again. Heat half the oil in a wok and when very hot stir-fry peppers and onion for ¾ minute. Remove.
Add the black bean paste with ginger and fry briefly, then add remaining oil and the beef. Stir-fry on high heat until cooked through, about 2½ minutes.
Pour in the sauce, return peppers and onion, and stir until sauce is thickened and clear.

Serving:
Garnish with sliced tomato and cucumber.

Beef and Bamboo Shoots

375 g (¾ lb) fillet or frying steak
2 tablespoons meat marinade
2 teaspoons cornflour
185 g (6 oz) canned bamboo shoots, drained
2 shallots (or 1 small onion)
2 slices fresh ginger
1 clove garlic
3 tablespoons vegetable oil
Sauce:
6 tablespoons beef stock or consomme
2 teaspoons dry sherry
½ teaspoon sesame oil
½ teaspoon cornflour
pinch each of salt and white pepper

Preparation:
Slice well-chilled beef thinly across the grain, then cut into bite-sized squares. Season with marinade and cornflour and leave for 45 minutes.
Thinly slice bamboo shoots, shallots or onion and shred ginger and garlic.
Mix sauce ingredients in a bowl.

Cooking:
Heat oil in a wok and when very hot put in drained beef with garlic and stir-fry on high heat until lightly coloured, about 1½ minutes. Lift out and keep warm.
Add shallot or onion, ginger and bamboo shoot and stir-fry for 1½ minutes, then pour in the sauce and bring to the boil. Return meat and simmer until sauce thickens and clears, and meat is tender.

Serving:
Garnish with shredded green and red chilli.

Chinese Cabbage with Asparagus

12 spears canned asparagus, drained
625 g (1¼ lb) Chinese or celery cabbage
3 cups water
1 tablespoon chicken stock powder
2 teaspoons light soy sauce
2 teaspoons dry sherry
1 teaspoon sugar
3 tablespoons rendered chicken fat or lard

Preparation:
Cut asparagus into 2.5cm (1″) pieces.
Rinse cabbage in cold water, separate leaves and cut into pieces about 5cm (2″) square.
Cut hard stems into diagonal slices.

Cooking:
Bring water to the boil, add stock powder and drop in the cabbage stems. Boil for 1½ minutes, then add leaves and boil for ½ minute. Lift out and drain well, reserving a little of the liquid.
Heat chicken fat or lard in a wok and stir-fry cabbage on high heat for ½ minute. Add asparagus with soy sauce, sherry and sugar and stir carefully on moderate heat for ½ minute. Pour in about 3 tablespoons of the reserved stock thickened with ½ teaspoon cornflour and bring to the boil. Simmer until the sauce thickens.

Serving:
Arrange vegetables on a serving plate and spoon on the sauce.

Fried Bamboo Shoots with Dried Scallops

375 g (¾ lb) canned bamboo shoots, drained
2 tablespoons light soy sauce
1 heaped tablespoon sugar
2 teaspoons sesame oil
3 dried sea scallops (or 30g/1 oz dried fish)
1 large bunch fresh parsley
2 teaspoons sugar
deep-frying oil

Preparation:
Cut bamboo shoots into pieces about 5cm × 1.25cm (2″ × ½″). Place in a plastic bag and pour in soy sauce, sugar and sesame oil. Secure top and shake well. Leave to marinate for 45 minutes, turning bag occasionally.
Boil scallops in a little water until tender, then shred. Drain bamboo shoots and wipe dry.

Cooking:
Heat deep-frying oil to very hot in a wok or saucepan, reduce heat slightly and put in the bamboo shoots.
Deep-fry for 3½-4 minutes until lightly browned. Lift out and drain well.
Place shredded scallop in a wire strainer or perforated ladle and deep-fry until crisp, about 45 seconds. Drain on absorbent paper.
Remove parsley stems and drop the bunch into the hot oil. Cover pan to avoid spluttering, and leave to fry for about 20 seconds, shaking the pan gently during cooking. Lift out and drain very well.

Serving:
Arrange parsley on a serving plate and pile bamboo shoots on top. Scatter the fried scallop over the dish.

Note:
If using dried fish, cut into small pieces before deep-frying and crumble when cool.

Sliced Beef with Hot Peppers, page 44 ▶

Prawn Egg Foo Yung

6 large eggs
½ teaspoon salt
½ teaspoon sugar
¼ teaspoon white pepper
½ teaspoon sesame oil
2 tablespoons water
1½ teaspoons cornflour
250 g (½ lb) raw prawns, peeled
45 g (1½ oz) canned bamboo shoots, drained
1 shallot
3 tablespoons vegetable oil

Preparation:
Break eggs into a bowl, add salt, sugar, pepper, sesame oil, water and cornflour and beat until well mixed. Leave for 10 minutes. Rinse prawns and wipe dry. Shred bamboo shoots and shallot.

Cooking:
Heat oil in a wok and stir-fry prawns until pink, but not completely cooked through, about 1½ minutes. Lift out and set aside. Add bamboo shoots and shallot and stir-fry for 1 minute, then return prawns. Pour in the egg mixture and mix well with the prawns and vegetables. Reduce heat to moderately low, cover and cook until the underside is firm enough to turn. Cut into quarters, turn and raise heat to cook the other side to a golden brown.

Serving:
Lift onto a serving plate, overlapping the pieces. Garnish with fresh coriander or parsley and sliced tomato.

Chicken and Chinese Sausage in a Rice Pot

375 g (¾ lb) medium grain white rice
4 dried black mushrooms, soaked
375 g (¾ lb) chicken, boneless
1½ tablespoons poultry marinade
1 teaspoon cornflour
½ teaspoon sesame oil
2 dried Chinese sausages
6 stems Chinese cabbage or Choy Sum
2 slices fresh ginger
3½ cups water
1 heaped tablespoon chicken stock powder

Preparation:
Wash rice and drain well.
Squeeze water from mushrooms, remove stems and slice thinly. Skin chicken and cut into bite-sized pieces. Season with marinade, cornflour and sesame oil and leave for 15 minutes.
Wash Chinese sausages and cut into 2cm (¾″) diagonal slices. Rinse vegetables in cold water and cut in two or three pieces. Shred ginger.

Cooking:
Pour rice into a rice cooker or heavy based saucepan, adding water and stock powder. Cover and bring to the boil.
Reduce heat and simmer until the liquid is level with the rice. Place mushrooms, chicken, sausage and vegetables on the rice and scatter on shredded ginger.
Cover and cook on low heat until rice is cooked and meat and vegetables are tender.

Serving:
Stir meat and vegetables evenly into the rice and serve in the cooking pot or transfer to a deep, covered dish. Serve with a bowl of chilli or soy sauce.

Noodles with Crabmeat in Soup

250 g (½ lb) thin 'E mein' noodles
2 egg whites
250 g (½ lb) fresh beanshoots
250 g (½ lb) frozen, fresh or canned crabmeat
1 shallot
8 cups water
2 tablespoons chicken stock powder
2 tablespoons vegetable oil
salt

Preparation:
Soak noodles in warm water to soften.
Loosen the bundles and drain well.
Lightly beat egg whites and set aside.
Rinse beanshoots in cold water. Remove roots and pods, if preferred. Flake crabmeat and shred shallot.

Cooking:
Bring water to the boil and add chicken stock. Add noodles and simmer on moderate heat for 3 minutes.
Add flaked crabmeat and shallot and simmer for 1 more minute, then season with salt to taste.
Remove from the heat and pour in egg white. Leave until the egg sets in white threads in the soup, then stir and reheat gently.
Heat oil in a wok and stir-fry beanshoots until softened, but retaining crispness. Add to the soup.

Serving:
Serve soup in a large tureen or covered dish, adding a little sesame oil and white pepper to taste.

Fried Bamboo Shoots with Dried Scallops, page 46 ▶

90 g (3 oz) rice stick noodles
250 g (½ lb) frozen or fresh sea scallops
125 g (¼ lb) frozen or fresh lobster meat (or
  use additional prawns)
185 g (6 oz) raw medium prawns, peeled
½ green pepper
1 shallot
6 slices ginger
30 g (1 oz) Chinese pickles or preserved
  Chow Chow
½ fresh red chilli
deep-frying oil
Sauce:
½ cup water
1 teaspoon chicken stock powder
1 tablespoon light soy sauce
2 teaspoons dry sherry
½ teaspoon sugar
¾ teaspoon cornflour
pinch each of salt and white pepper

Preparation:
Thaw and rinse frozen scallops and lobster,
if used, cut into bite-sized pieces.
Slit down centre backs of prawns and
remove dark veins. Rinse in cold water and
cut each into three pieces.
Cut pepper and shallot into long shreds and
shred ginger. Shred pickles or Chow Chow if
pieces are large. Shred chilli. Mix sauce
ingredients in a bowl.

Cooking:
Heat deep oil to very hot in a wok or
saucepan and then reduce heat slightly.
Drop in handfuls of the broken rice stick
noodles and cook for a few seconds until
they expand and float to the surface.
Remove before they begin to colour. Drain
well and arrange on a serving plate. Drop
seafood into the oil and deep-fry for ½
minute, then remove and keep warm.
Pour off all but 2½ tablespoons oil and stir-
fry pepper, shallot and ginger for 1 minute.
Return the seafood and stir-fry for ½
minute, then pour in the sauce and bring to
the boil.
Stir until sauce begins to clear, then add
pickles or Chow Chow and chilli. Mix
thoroughly. Heat for ½ minute.

Serving:
Spoon seafood over the noodles and garnish
with parsley and sliced cucumber.

From the East

Food from the East, especially from the city of Shanghai and its neighbouring countryside, is noted for its rich tastes. Dishes are well-seasoned with garlic and the pungent sesame oil. They are warming, substantial and quite oily. Therefore, a variety of steamed breads is served in preference to rice, to soak up the oily excess.

In contrast to the more lavish Northern Peking cuisine, the food of the East might be called home-style cooking, exemplified by such dishes as Braised Brown Sauce Duck and Crisp Fried Pork Chops.

Some of the finest seafood dishes served in China originated along the Eastern Fukien coast and the great Yangtze River, whose mouth is at Shanghai. River carp, clams, sea cucumbers (or more accurately, sea slugs), eels and the delicately flavoured Shanghai hairy crab, a true gourmet food, are found on most Eastern menus. They are invariably cooked with strong and distinct seasonings which do not camouflage, but rather highlight the natural flavours.

The range of Eastern vegetable dishes is great. Favourites are Chinese cabbage, cooked with a creamy sauce and broad beans or green beans stir-fried with chopped ham or sesame seeds.

And when it comes to noodles, the Eastern style is a thick, spaghetti-like wheat flour noodle which is traditionally cooked with shredded vegetables and pork and flavoured with a brown sauce. A plate of these is a meal in itself, but they are most often served as the final dish in an already very filling meal.

Cubed Fish with Broccoli ▶

500 g (1 lb) meaty white fish fillets
1 tablespoon seafood marinade
1 tablespoon cornflour
½ teaspoon sesame oil (optional)
2 cloves garlic
1 shallot
2 slices fresh ginger
250 g (½ lb) fresh broccoli
3 slices fresh ginger
1 tablespoon dry sherry
pinch of bicarbonate of soda
4 tablespoons oil
Sauce:
⅓ cup water
½ teaspoon chicken stock powder
2 teaspoons dry sherry
¼ teaspoon sesame oil
½ teaspoon cornflour
pinch each of salt and white pepper

Preparation:
Cut meat into 2.5cm (1") cubes and season with marinade, cornflour and sesame oil, if used. Leave for 10 minutes.
Mince garlic, cut shallot into 2cm (¾") pieces and shred ginger.
Break broccoli into florets and rinse well. Drain.
Mix sauce ingredients in a bowl.

Cooking:
Bring a small saucepan of water to the boil. Add 3 slices ginger, sherry and bicarbonate of soda. Add the broccoli and boil for 2½ minutes, then drain, splash with cold water to brighten the colour and drain again. Set aside.
Heat oil in a wok and when very hot, stir-fry garlic, shallot and ginger for ½ minute. Add fish cubes and stir-fry on high heat for 1 minute.
Reduce heat slightly and cook until the fish is done, stirring continually, about 2 more minutes.
Pour in the sauce and boil until thickened and glazing the fish. Add broccoli and reheat briefly.

Serving:
Arrange broccoli around the edge of a plate and pile the fish in the centre.

Barbecue Sauce Fish

750 g (1½ lb) whole bream or flounder
1 shallot
4 slices fresh ginger
3 cloves garlic
2 tablespoons Hoisin or barbecue sauce
3 tablespoons vegetable oil
Sauce:
¾ cup fish stock or water
1 tablespoon light soy sauce
1 tablespoon dry sherry
1 tablespoon Worcester sauce
2-3 teaspoons sugar
1½ teaspoons cornflour
pinch each of salt and white pepper

Preparation:
Clean fish, wash and wipe dry. Score diagonally across the body on both sides at 2.5cm (1") intervals.
Mince shallot, ginger and garlic and mix with Hoisin or barbecue sauce and oil.
Mix sauce ingredients in a bowl.

Cooking:
Heat a wok and stir-fry the sauce and shallot mixture for 1 minute on moderately high heat. Add the fish and reduce heat slightly. Simmer for 2 minutes, turning once, and basting frequently with the sauce.
Add pre-mixed sauce and bring to the boil. Cover and cook on moderate heat until the fish is tender, about 6 minutes. Turn fish once, and baste frequently.

Serving:
Lift carefully onto a serving plate and cover with the sauce. Garnish with fresh coriander or parsley.

Braised Yellow Fish

750 g (1½ lb) yellow fish or snapper (or 2
    smaller fish)
2 tablespoons seafood marinade
2 egg whites
3 tablespoons cornflour
45 g (1½ oz) fat pork (optional)
2 shallots (or 1 small onion)
2 cloves garlic
3 dried black mushrooms, soaked
30 g (1 oz) canned bamboo shoots, drained
deep-frying oil
Sauce:
1½ cups fish stock or water
1 tablespoon dark soy sauce
2 teaspoons dry sherry
1 teaspoon sugar
1 teaspoon sesame oil (optional)
1 teaspoon cornflour
pinch of white pepper

Preparation:
Clean fish, and wipe dry. Score diagonally
across the body on both sides at 2.5cm (1″)
intervals. Season with marinade and leave
20 minutes.
Lightly beat egg whites. Shred fat pork, if
used.
Finely shred shallot or slice onion, shred
garlic, black mushrooms and bamboo
shoots.
Mix sauce ingredients in a bowl.

Cooking:
Heat deep oil to very hot in a large wok,
then reduce heat slightly. Brush fish with egg
whites, then coat thickly with cornflour and
deep-fry until lightly coloured and half
cooked through. Turn once only.
Lift out and keep warm.
Drain off all but 3 tablespoons oil and stir-
fry pork with shallots or onions, garlic,
mushrooms and bamboo shoots on
moderate heat for 3 minutes.
Add sauce and bring to the boil, then
simmer for 3 minutes.
Return fish, baste well with the sauce and
braise, covered, for about 4 minutes.

Serving:
Carefully lift fish onto a serving plate and
spoon on the sauce and vegetables.
Season with extra sesame oil and plenty of
white pepper and garnish with slivers of
young ginger.

Abalone with Oyster Sauce

500 g (1 lb) canned abalone, drained
500 g (1 lb) fresh lettuce
1 teaspoon sesame oil
2 tablespoons vegetable oil
Sauce:
1 cup water
¾ teaspoon chicken stock powder
1 tablespoon dark soy sauce
3 tablespoons oyster sauce
1 tablespoon dry sherry
½ teaspoon salt
2 teaspoons sugar
1 teaspoon cornflour

Preparation:
Cut abalone into very thin slices,
horizontally.
Separate lettuce leaves and wash well.
Drain.
Mix sauce ingredients in a bowl.

Cooking:
Dip lettuce leaves into a pot of boiling
water, remove, drain and arrange on a
serving plate. Sprinkle with sesame oil and
half the vegetable oil and set aside.
Simmer abalone in the stock for 1 minute,
then drain.
Heat remaining oil and pour in the sauce.
Bring to the boil, then reduce heat and add
sliced abalone.
Simmer gently for 2 minutes.

Serving:
Arrange abalone on the lettuce and spoon
on the sauce.
Sprinkle with additional sesame oil and
white pepper.

Clams in Bean Sauce

1 kg (2 lb) fresh clams, in shells (or use
    mussels)
2 shallots (or 1 small onion)
6-8 cloves garlic
3 tablespoons vegetable oil
Sauce:
½ cup water
½ teaspoon chicken stock powder
1½ tablespoons canned salted yellow beans
    in sauce
2 teaspoons dry sherry
2 teaspoons sugar
1 teaspoon cornflour

Preparation:
Wash clams (or mussels) well, brush with a
stiff brush under cold water and rinse.
Chop shallots or onion, and garlic finely.
Mix sauce ingredients in a bowl.

Cooking:
Heat oil in a large wok and add clams (or
mussels) with onion and garlic. Cover and
shake pan over moderately high heat until
shells open.
Add bean sauce and bring to the boil.
Simmer for 1½ minutes.

Serving:
Pick out shells which have not opened.
Discard.
Transfer clams to a deep serving dish.

Note:
Add chopped red or green chilli during
cooking, for a hotter dish.

"Drunk Chicken"

2 kg (4 lb) plump chicken
2-3 tablespoons salt
2½ cups 'Shao Hsing' Chinese wine, or dry
   sherry
1 cup well-flavoured chicken stock

Preparation:
Clean chicken, wash and wipe dry.

Cooking:
Place chicken in a fireproof casserole and set in a steamer.
Cover tightly and steam over moderately high heat for 1 hour.
Remove from the heat and leave to cool in the steamer.
Lift chicken out, joint and coat each piece with salt.
Arrange the salted chicken pieces in another, lightly oiled glass casserole. Cover and refrigerate for at least 5 hours.
Heat wine or sherry with chicken stock to almost boiling.
Pour over the chicken. Cover again and return to the refrigerator for 1-2 days.

Serving:
Cut the chilled chicken into bite-sized pieces and arrange on a plate. Surround with pickled cucumber or radish.
Serve as an appetiser or main dish.

Pickled Cucumber And Radish

fresh cucumber and/or radish
white vinegar
salt
sugar

Preparation:
Wash cucumber and peel radish. Cut into 2cm (¾") cubes and place in a jar or bowl. Mix 2 parts white vinegar with 1 part water, adding salt and sugar to taste. Pour over the vegetables, cover and leave for 1 day. Drain before using.
Add finely chopped red chilli or crushed peppercorns for a hotter pickle.

Chicken Wrapped in Paper ▶

500 g (1 lb) chicken, boneless
1½ teaspoons five spices powder
1½ teaspoons salt
2 teaspoons sesame oil
60 g (2 oz) pork fat
3 dried black mushrooms, soaked
12 sprigs fresh coriander or parsley
1 fresh red chilli
cellophane, greaseproof or edible rice paper
deep-frying oil

Preparation:
Skin chicken and cut into thin slices. Season with five spices, salt and sesame oil, rubbing well in.
Squeeze water from mushrooms, remove stems and slice thinly.
Cut chilli into thin slices.
Cut paper into 20cm (8") squares.
Place pork fat on a saucer and set in a steamer to cook over rapidly boiling water for 15 minutes. Slice into 12 pieces.
Arrange several slices of chicken, a slice of pork fat, several strips of mushroom, a piece of coriander or parsley and several pieces of chilli in the centre of each paper square. Draw into a bundle and tie with cotton, or fold into an envelope shape, tucking the end flap in securely.

Cooking:
Heat deep oil to very hot, then reduce heat slightly.
Put in wrapped chicken, several packages at a time, to deep-fry for 2½-3 minutes. Remove and drain well.

Serving:
Snip the cotton and arrange parcels on a plate with fresh coriander or parsley to garnish.

Walnut Chicken

500 g (1 lb) chicken breasts
2 egg whites
2 tablespoons cornflour
2 teaspoons dry sherry
2 teaspoons spicy salt
185 g (6 oz) shelled walnuts
deep-frying oil

Preparation:
Skin chicken and cut each breast into three or four slices. Flatten by batting several times on each side with the flat side of a cleaver.
Season with egg whites, cornflour, sherry and spicy salt and leave for 25 minutes, turning occasionally.
Drop walnuts into a pan of boiling water and cook until the skins loosen. Drain and cool slightly, then rub off skins and leave nuts to dry. Chop finely.

Cooking:
Heat deep oil to very hot, reduce heat slightly.
Coat the chicken steaks thickly with chopped walnuts, pressing on firmly. Place, several at a time, in the hot oil and fry to a golden brown. Remove and drain.

Serving:
Arrange walnut chicken on paper napkins on a serving plate and garnish with pickled ginger and cubes of pineapple.
Serve with dips of spicy salt and soy sauce.

Sweet and Sour Duck with Ginger, page 58 ▶

Sweet and Sour Duck with Ginger

500 g (1 lb) duckling pieces
2½ tablespoons poultry marinade
2 tablespoons Hoisin sauce
4 slices canned pineapple, drained
8 slices young fresh ginger, or preserved
   ginger
1 shallot
3 tablespoons oil
Sauce:
¼ cup water
½ teaspoon chicken stock powder
⅔ cup pineapple juice
1 tablespoon light soy sauce
1 tablespoon tomato paste
1½ tablespoons white vinegar
1 tablespoon sugar (or to taste)
1 tablespoon vegetable oil
1 teaspoon cornflour

Preparation:
Place duckling pieces in a fireproof dish and season with marinade and Hoisin sauce.
Cut pineapple into wedges and shred ginger and shallot.
Mix sauce ingredients in a small saucepan.

Cooking:
Set duckling in a steamer and cook over rapidly boiling water until tender, about 20 minutes. Lift out and leave to cool.
Bring sauce to the boil and simmer, stirring, until thickened. Chop duckling into bite-sized pieces.
Heat oil in a wok and when very hot, stir-fry duck with shallot for 2 minutes. Add ginger and pineapple and stir-fry on high heat for 1 more minute. Pour in the sauce and return to the boil. Simmer until thickened and clear.

Serving:
Arrange the duck on a plate and add pineapple and ginger. Spoon on the sauce. Surround with slices of pineapple topped with maraschino cherries.

Braised Brown Sauce Duck

2½ kg (5 lb) duck
⅓ cup dark soy sauce
1½ teaspoons five spices powder
3 shallots (or 1 medium onion)
3-4 slices fresh ginger
1 whole star anise (optional)
¼ cup dry sherry
90 g (3 oz) brown sugar or honey
2 teaspoons salt
2 teaspoons sesame oil
250 g (½ lb) Chinese cabbage or spinach
deep-frying oil

Preparation:
Clean duck, wash and wipe dry. Place in a dish and pour on soy sauce. Rub well into the skin and inside the cavity, then season with five spices powder, rubbing in well.
Cover and leave for 45 minutes.
Shred shallots or thinly slice onion. Shred ginger and crumble star anise.

Cooking:
Heat deep-oil, enough to half-cover the duck, to very hot and then reduce heat slightly.
Check that there is no liquid in the cavity of the duck.
Lower into the oil to deep-fry until well coloured with skin very crisp. Turn several times during cooking to colour evenly. Remove and drain well.

Pour off all but 4 tablespoons oil and stir-fry shallot or onion and ginger for 1 minute. Return the duck, add star anise, if used, and cover with boiling water. Cover the pan and bring to the boil, then reduce heat and braise gently until duck is very tender, 2-2½ hours. Add sherry, sugar or honey, salt and any reserved soy sauce marinade after first 1 hour of cooking.
Sprinkle on sesame oil when duck is done. The sauce should have reduced to about 1 cup.
Blanch spinach or Chinese cabbage in boiling water for a few seconds, then drain well and stir-fry with 2 tablespoons vegetable oil for 1½-2 minutes, adding a pinch of salt and sugar.

Serving:
Arrange the vegetables on a large serving plate. Slice duck and pile on the vegetables. Pour on the sauce.

Lion's Head Meatballs

▶

750 g (1½ lb) minced lean pork
125 g (¼ lb) transparent bean thread
   vermicelli
250 g (½ lb) celery cabbage or spinach
water or beef stock
shallow-frying oil
Seasonings:
2 tablespoons dark soy sauce
1½ tablespoons dry sherry
8 slices fresh ginger
3 shallots (or 1 medium onion)
1 tablespoon cornflour
Sauce:
2 tablespoons dark soy sauce
2 tablespoons sweet bean paste or Hoisin
   sauce
1½ teaspoons salt
2 teaspoons sugar

Preparation:
Grind minced pork in a large mortar or blender with the seasoning ingredients, until the mixture is smooth and lump-free.
Form into several large meatballs, about 8cm (3″) in diameter. Set aside.
Soak vermicelli in warm water to soften.
Cut cabbage into 10cm (4″) squares
Remove spinach stems, if used.
Mix sauce ingredients in a bowl.

Cooking:
Heat shallow oil (about 5cm/2″) in a wok and when very hot reduce heat slightly. Put in meatballs to fry until evenly coloured, turning carefully from time to time. Lift out and drain well.
Pour off all but 3 tablespoons oil and stir-fry vegetables for 1½ minutes. Arrange in the bottom of a casserole and top with the drained vermicelli. Place the meatballs on top.
Pour in the sauce and add water or beef stock to half cover the meatballs.
Cover the casserole and cook in a moderate oven for 45 minutes. The liquid should be well absorbed into the meatballs and noodles.

Serving:
Serve in the casserole.

Crisp Fried Pork Chops

750 g (1½ lb) small lean pork chops
4 cloves garlic
2 egg whites
3 tablespoons cornflour
¾ teaspoon salt
deep-frying oil
Seasoning:
1 tablespoon dark soy sauce
2 teaspoons dry sherry
1 teaspoon white vinegar
2 teaspoons sugar
¾ teaspoon five spices powder
pinch of white pepper

Preparation:
Trim chops and place in a dish. Mix seasonings and pour over the chops. Leave for 15 minutes.
Crush garlic and mix with lightly beaten egg whites, cornflour and salt.
Pour over the chops and leave for a further 20 minutes, turning occasionally.

Cooking:
Heat deep oil to very hot and deep-fry chops, several at a time, until dark brown and well crisped, about 3 minutes or longer if chops are large.
Lift out and drain well.
Re-fry briefly in very hot oil before serving.

Serving:
Cover a plate with shredded lettuce and arrange chops on top. Serve with a spicy salt dip.

Spicy Salt

4 tablespoons table salt
1 teaspoon five spices powder

Preparation:
Pour salt into a dry wok and stir constantly on moderate heat until it takes on a light colour. Remove from the heat and stir in five spices powder. Leave to cool.
Pour into a screw-top jar to store. Shake well and use as needed.

Braised Spareribs

750 g (1½ lb) lean pork spareribs
2 tablespoons salted black beans
5 cloves garlic
3 shallots (or 1 medium onion)
5 slices fresh ginger
½ cup dark soy sauce
1 tablespoon dry sherry
2-2½ tablespoons sugar or honey
1½ cups water
1 teaspoon chicken stock powder
3 tablespoons vegetable oil

Preparation:
Divide ribs and cut into 5cm (2″) pieces.
Lightly crush black beans with garlic and finely chop shallots or onion and ginger.

Cooking:
Heat oil in a wok and stir-fry the ribs on high heat for 3 minutes, until beginning to colour. Add black bean and garlic paste, chopped shallots or onion, and ginger. Stir-fry until ribs are well coloured, adding a little water or oil if pan becomes dry.
Add soy sauce, sherry and sugar or honey. Mix well and cook for 1 more minute. Pour in the water and sprinkle on chicken stock. Bring to the boil, then reduce heat and cover. Simmer until ribs are completely tender and sauce reduced, about 30 minutes.

Serving:
Arrange ribs on a serving plate and pour on the sauce. Garnish with finely chopped shallot or coriander.

Note:
Add finely chopped red chilli during cooking for extra taste.

Beef in Barbecue Sauce

500 g (1 lb) fillet or frying steak
3 tablespoons meat marinade
2 teaspoons cornflour
3 cloves garlic
3 slices fresh ginger
1 small onion
3 tablespoons vegetable oil
Sauce:
½ cup beef stock or consomme
1 tablespoon dark soy sauce
2 tablespoons Hoisin or barbecue sauce
1 tablespoon tomato sauce
1 teaspoon white vinegar
2 teaspoons sugar
1 teaspoon cornflour

Preparation:
Slice well-chilled beef thinly across the grain, then cut into 2cm (¾″) strips. Season with marinade and cornflour and leave for 45 minutes.
Slice garlic, shred ginger and thinly slice onion.
Mix sauce ingredients in a bowl.

Cooking:
Heat oil in a wok and fry garlic briefly, then add drained beef and stir-fry on high heat for 2½ minutes. Lift out and keep warm.
Add ginger and onion and stir-fry for 1½ minutes. Remove.
Pour in the sauce and bring to the boil, reduce heat slightly and when sauce begins to thicken, return beef, ginger and onion and heat through.

Serving:
Arrange on a plate and sprinkle with a little sesame oil.

Oyster Sauce Beef

500 g (1 lb) frying steak
4 tablespoons meat marinade
2 teaspoons cornflour
2 shallots (or 1 small onion)
3 slices fresh ginger
8 dried black mushrooms, soaked
4 tablespoons vegetable oil
Sauce:
⅓ cup water
2 teaspoons dark soy sauce
3 tablespoons oyster sauce
1½ teaspoons sugar
¾ teaspoon cornflour

Preparation:
Slice well-chilled beef across the grain, then cut into 4cm (1½") squares. Season with marinade and cornflour and leave for at least 45 minutes. To make more tender, pound with the blunt edge of the cleaver until flattened.
Cut shallots into 2cm (¾") pieces or onion into squares. Shred ginger. Squeeze water from mushrooms, remove stems and place the whole mushrooms on a plate in a steamer.
Mix sauce ingredients in a bowl.

Cooking:
Steam mushrooms over rapidly boiling water for 8 minutes.
Heat oil in a wok and when very hot, fry drained beef for 2½ minutes on high heat. Lift out and set aside.
Add shallots or onion and stir-fry for 1 minute, then add ginger and mushrooms and stir-fry for 1 more minute on moderate heat.
Return meat and pour in the reserved marinade and sauce.
Simmer, stirring, until sauce thickens.

Serving:
Arrange meat with mushrooms on top, on a serving plate.
Spoon on the sauce and garnish with finely chopped shallot or parsley.

Braised Beef with Beancurd and Vegetables ▶

500 g (1 lb) lean frying steak
2½ tablespoons meat marinade
1½ teaspoons cornflour
1 teaspoon sesame oil (optional)
6 dried black mushrooms, soaked
90 g (3 oz) canned bamboo shoots, drained
60 g (2 oz) frozen green peas, green beans or snow peas
60 g (2 oz) canned button mushrooms, drained
1 medium carrot
1 large onion
3 cloves garlic
½ fresh red chilli
10 cubes fried beancurd
4 tablespoons vegetable oil
Sauce:
1 cup water
1 teaspoon chicken stock powder
1 tablespoon dark soy sauce
2 tablespoons oyster sauce
1 teaspoon white vinegar
2 teaspoons sugar
1 teaspoon sesame oil
1½ teaspoons cornflour
pinch of white pepper

Preparation:
Slice well-chilled beef fairly thickly across the grain, then cut into bite-sized cubes. Season with marinade, cornflour and sesame oil, if used, and leave for 45 minutes. Squeeze water from mushrooms, remove stems and slice.
Slice bamboo shoots and carrot. Cut beans, if used, into 4cm (1½") pieces and drop into boiling water to parboil for 1 minute. If using frozen peas thaw in boiling water and drain, or if using snowpeas, remove strings and rinse.
Cut large button mushrooms in halves, horizontally.
Cut onion into 2cm (¾") squares.
Slice garlic and shred ginger.
Mix sauce ingredients in a bowl.

Cooking:
Heat oil in a wok and fry beancurd cubes on moderate heat for 2-3 minutes. Remove and drain.
Add garlic and fry briefly, then add drained beef and stir-fry on high heat for 2 minutes. Remove and keep warm.
Stir-fry vegetables for 1½ minutes, then pour in the sauce.
Bring to the boil, return meat and beancurd, cover and braise on moderate heat until the sauce thickens and meat, beancurd and vegetables are tender.

Serving:
Garnish with finely chopped coriander and shallot.

Note:
Add garlic and chilli sauce, to taste, for a hotter dish.

Bean Salad

500 g (1 lb) green beans, broad beans or lima beans
2 teaspoons white sesame seeds
½ teaspoon salt
2 teaspoons sesame oil
3 tablespoons vegetable oil

Preparation:
Cut beans into 5cm (2") pieces, if used.

Cooking:
Lightly toast sesame seeds until they begin to pop, then set aside.
Parboil broad or lima beans, if used, until the skins loosen. Drain and rub off skins.
Bring a saucepan of water to the boil. Add salt and 1 tablespoon of the oil and boil beans until almost tender. Drain well.
Heat oil in a wok and when very hot stir-fry the beans until cooked through, but still crisp.

Serving:
Place beans in a salad bowl or serving dish and sprinkle with sesame oil and toasted sesame seeds. Serve warm or cold.

Note:
Use finely chopped crisp-fried bacon or shredded fried dried scallop in place of sesame seeds.

Chop Suey Chicken

375 g (¾ lb) chicken, boneless
1½ tablespoons poultry marinade
2 teaspoons cornflour
125 g (¼ lb) fresh beanshoots
125 g (¼ lb) snow peas or green beans
45 g (1½ oz) canned bamboo shoots, drained
1 small carrot
1 large onion
8 canned water chestnuts, drained
8 cobs canned baby corn, drained
1 fresh red chilli, (optional)
8 stalks Chinese green vegetables (optional)
deep-frying oil
Sauce:
¾ cup water
2 teaspoons chicken stock powder
2 teaspoons light soy sauce
2 teaspoons dry sherry
2 teaspoons cornflour
pinch each of sugar, salt and white pepper

Preparation:
Cut chilled chicken into 2cm (¾") cubes.
Season with marinade and cornflour and
leave for 20 minutes.
Rinse beanshoots in cold water, drain and
remove pods and roots, if preferred. String
snow peas or beans. Cut beans, if used, into
5cm (2") pieces.
Thinly slice bamboo shoots and carrot. Cut
onion into 2cm (¾") squares. Slice water
chestnuts horizontally.
Cut large baby corn cobs in halves. Slice
chilli.
Wash and trim Chinese vegetables, if used,
and cut into 5cm (2") pieces.
Mix sauce ingredients in a bowl.

Cooking:
Heat deep oil to moderately hot and fry
chicken until white and almost cooked
through, about 1¼ minutes. Lift out and
drain well.
Pour off all but 3 tablespoons oil and stir-fry
vegetables, except Chinese vegetables and
beanshoots, for 2 minutes. Return chicken
and add the sauce.
Cover and bring to the boil. Simmer for 2
minutes.
Add beanshoots and cook, stirring, on
moderate heat until softened.
Add finely chopped chilli for extra taste.
Keep warm.
Blanch the Chinese vegetable in boiling
water for 1½ minutes.
Drain and stir-fry in 2 tablespoons oil on
high heat for about 2 minutes, until tender.

Serving:
Pile the chop suey in the centre of a serving
plate and sprinkle on sesame oil and
chopped shallot. Surround with the green
vegetables.

Baby Corn and Mushrooms

12 large dried black mushrooms, soaked
3 cups water
1 tablespoon chicken stock powder
410 g (13 oz) can baby corn cobs, drained
1 shallot
3 slices fresh ginger
3 tablespoons vegetable oil
Sauce:
1 tablespoon dark soy sauce
2 tablespoons oyster sauce
1 tablespoon dry sherry
1½ teaspoons sugar
1 teaspoon sesame oil
1 teaspoon cornflour

Preparation:
Squeeze water from mushrooms, remove
stems and place caps in a saucepan with
water and stock powder.
Cut large corn cobs in halves.
Shred shallot and ginger.
Mix sauce ingredients in a bowl.

Cooking:
Bring stock to the boil, then reduce heat and
simmer mushrooms for 10 minutes. Add
baby corn and simmer for 10 more minutes.
Drain, reserving ½ cup of the liquid.
Heat oil in a wok and when very hot, stir-fry
shallot and ginger for 1 minute. Add
mushrooms and stir-fry on high heat for ½
minute, then add the baby corn and stir-fry
briefly.
Pour in the sauce and bring to the boil,
adding reserved cooking liquid.
Simmer until the sauce thickens.

Serving:
Transfer vegetables to a plate and spoon on
the sauce.
Garnish with fresh coriander or parsley.

Cabbage in Cream Sauce

750 g (1½ lb) celery cabbage
3 rashers streaky bacon
1 tablespoon dry sherry
3 tablespoons vegetable oil
Sauce:
⅓ cup water
1½ teaspoons chicken stock powder
½ cup fresh milk
¾ teaspoon salt
2 teaspoons cornflour

Preparation:
Separate cabbage leaves and rinse well in
cold water. Trim off the thick bases of outer
leaves.
Finely chop bacon and fry in its own fat
until very crisp.
Mix sauce ingredients in a bowl.

Cooking:
Bring a pot of water to the boil and drop in
cabbage. Boil until stems have softened,
about 2 minutes then lift out and drain well.
Heat oil in a wok and stir-fry cabbage on
high heat for ½-¾ minute.
Add sherry and stir-fry for ½ minute more,
then pour in the sauce and bring to the boil.
Simmer until thickened.

Serving:
Arrange the vegetables on a serving plate
and cover with the sauce. Sprinkle crisp
bacon on top.

Braised Vegetables with Beancurd

12 dried black mushrooms
2 squares pressed beancurd
60 g (2 oz) green beans
60 g (2 oz) canned bamboo shoots, drained
60 g (2 oz) canned lotus root, drained
1 medium carrot
2 stalks celery
1 medium onion
125 g (¼ lb) Chinese cabbage
90 g (3 oz) snow peas or fresh beanshoots
4 tablespoons vegetable oil
Sauce:
1¼ cups liquid from soaked mushrooms
2 tablespoons light soy sauce
1 tablespoon Hoisin sauce or sweet bean paste
1½ teaspoons sugar
1 teaspoon sesame oil
2-3 points star anise
2 teaspoons cornflour
pinch of white pepper

Preparation:
Soak mushrooms in 2 cups boiling water for ½ hour.
Drain, reserving liquid for the sauce.
Cut beancurd into 2cm (¾″) cubes, rinse with cold water and drain.
Slice beans, bamboo shoots, lotus root, carrot, celery and cut onion into 2cm (¾″) squares.
Wash cabbage and cut into 5cm (2″) pieces, cutting thick stalks into diagonal slices.
Rinse and string snow peas, or remove pods and roots from beanshoots, if used.
Mix sauce ingredients in a bowl.

Cooking:
Heat oil in a large wok and fry beancurd cubes until lightly coloured. Lift out and set aside.
Add mushrooms and stir-fry for 2 minutes, then add celery, beans, carrot and onion and stir-fry for 1½ minutes.
Pour in the sauce and bring to the boil. Add bamboo shoots and lotus root. Cover and braise for 10 minutes.
Add the prepared cabbage and snowpeas or beanshoots, and fried beancurd. Stir on high heat for 2-3 minutes.

Serving:
Transfer to a deep serving dish and serve with chilli sauce.

Shanghai Noodles with Beanshoots

750 g (1½ lb) thick fresh noodles (or cooked spaghetti)
125 g (¼ lb) pork tenderloin (or chicken breast)
1 tablespoon pork or poultry marinade
125 g (¼ lb) raw baby shrimps, peeled
2 teaspoons cornflour
½ teaspoon salt
¼ teaspoon white pepper
185 g (6 oz) fresh beanshoots
2 stalks celery (optional)
2 cloves garlic
6 tablespoons vegetable oil
Sauce:
¼ cup water
¾ teaspoon chicken stock powder
1½ tablespoons dark soy sauce
1 tablespoon dry sherry
1 teaspoon salt
1 teaspoon sugar
¼ teaspoon white pepper
1 teaspoon sesame oil

Preparation:
Soak noodles in boiling water for 10 minutes. Drain.
Slice well chilled pork or chicken across the grain, then cut into fine shreds. Season with marinade and leave for 10 minutes. Rinse shrimps, pat dry and season with cornflour, salt and pepper. Leave for 7 minutes.
Rinse beanshoots and remove pods and roots. Cut celery, if used, into matchstick pieces. Slice garlic.
Mix sauce ingredients in a bowl.

Cooking:
Heat 2 tablespoons oil in a wok and stir-fry meat for 1½-2 minutes. Remove and add shrimps and stir-fry until pink, about 1 minute. Set aside.
Add 1 tablespoon more oil and fry beanshoots for 1-1½ minutes, then remove and add celery, if used, and garlic. Stir-fry until softened. Remove.
Wipe out the wok, add remaining oil and fry noodles, stirring until well coated with the oil and heated through.
Pour on the sauce and mix well. Return meat, shrimps and vegetables and mix thoroughly. Heat through, stirring constantly.

Serving:
Garnish with shredded omelette, wedges of tomato and parsley.

From the West

Western Chinese cooking — mainly the cooking of China's most heavily populated province, Szechwan — is most definitely for those who like it hot. The intense spiciness comes from the great quantities of chillies, garlic, ginger, Chinese brown peppercorns and the many hot chilli and preserved soy bean pastes that are used to season the food. Taste is so heavily stressed, that relatively little attention is paid to appearance.

It is said that in the olden days, the strong seasonings were for the purpose of warming the body against a rigorous climate and to ward off disease. And it is true that both garlic and ginger have a cleansing and beneficial effect on the digestive and circulatory systems, while chillies are loaded with vitamins A and C which, in other diets, would have been obtained from fresh fruit and vegetables.

More importantly, perhaps, was the fact that in this part of China, foodstuffs were scarce in any form, and rice made up the bulk of a meal. Therefore, what ingredients were available were treated to lashings of well-flavoured sauces to compensate for their meagre proportions.

But whatever the origins of the Szechwan cooking tradition, it is for certain the most unique in China. And, as its increasing popularity in the West shows, it is considered by many to be not just the most obviously tasty, but also the most fascinating.

Fish in Hot Tomato Sauce ▶

750 g (1½ lb) meaty fish fillets
2 tablespoons seafood marinade
2 egg whites
3 tablespoons cornflour
3 cloves garlic
1 medium onion
½ green pepper
2 shallots
5 slices fresh ginger
½-1 fresh red chilli
deep-frying oil
Sauce:
¾ cup water
1 teaspoon chicken stock powder
2 tablespoons tomato paste
2 tablespoons white vinegar
2 tablespoons sugar (or to taste)
1 teaspoon sesame oil
2 teaspoons cornflour
pinch each of salt and white pepper

Preparation:
Cut chilled fish into pieces about 4cm × 1cm (1½" × ¼") and season with marinade. Leave for 10 minutes.
Lightly beat egg whites, brush over fish, then coat with cornflour and leave for 10 more minutes.
Finely slice garlic, cut onion and peppers into 2cm (¾") squares and finely chop shallot. Shred ginger and chilli. Mix sauce ingredients in a bowl.

Cooking:
Bring a small pot of water to the boil and blanch pepper and onion for 20 seconds. Drain and splash with cold water to brighten colour. Drain again.
Heat 2 tablespoons oil in a wok and fry garlic briefly, then add pepper and onion squares and stir-fry for ½ minute. Add chopped shallot and shredded ginger and chilli and stir-fry for 1 minute. Pour in the sauce and bring to the boil. Simmer until thickened, then set aside.
In a large clean wok, heat deep oil to moderately hot and deep-fry fish until cooked through, about 1½ minutes. Drain off the oil. Pour in the sauce and heat through, or transfer fish to the other pan and heat through with the sauce.

Serving:
Arrange fish on a serving plate and top with vegetables and the sauce. Garnish with shredded shallot and red chilli.

Westlake Fish

750 g (1½ lb) bream, snapper or perch
3 slices fresh ginger
1 shallot
1 tablespoon dry sherry
10 cm (4") piece fresh ginger
3 dried black mushrooms, soaked
1-2 fresh red chillies
6 cups fish stock or water
1 teaspoon sesame oil (optional)
3 tablespoons vegetable oil
Sauce:
2 tablespoons dark soy sauce
2 tablespoons Worcester sauce
2 teaspoons tomato sauce
1½ tablespoons sugar
½ teaspoon salt
½ teaspoon black pepper
½ teaspoon cornflour

Preparation:
Clean fish and cut in halves along the backbone. Heat oil in a wok and gently fry on both sides until lightly coloured.
Arrange, meaty sides upwards, in a large flat casserole.
Finely shred sliced ginger and shallot and place on the fish. Sprinkle on sherry and leave for 10 minutes.
Shred the piece of ginger, mushrooms and chillies. Mix sauce ingredients in a small saucepan.

Cooking:
Bring stock to a rolling boil and add sesame oil, if used. Pour stock over the fish, cover and leave to gently poach in the hot stock for 10 minutes.
Steam shredded mushrooms for 10 minutes, adding ginger and chillies during last 3 minutes.
Lift fish onto a serving plate and scatter on mushrooms, ginger and chillies.
Bring sauce to the boil, adding about 3 tablespoons of the poaching liquid. Simmer until thickened.

Serving:
Pour sauce over the fish and garnish with fresh coriander.

Szechwan Chilli Prawns

750 g (1½ lb) raw prawns, in shells
3 tablespoons cornflour
3 shallots (or 1 medium onion)
45 g (1½ oz) canned bamboo shoots, drained
6 slices fresh ginger
4 cloves garlic
deep-frying oil
Sauce:
⅓ cup water
1 tablespoon dark soy sauce
½ cup tomato sauce
½-2 teaspoon chilli oil or chilli sauce
1 tablespoon dry sherry
1 teaspoon cornflour
pinch each of salt and white pepper

Preparation:
Remove heads and shells from prawns, leaving tails on. Slit down the centre backs, cutting almost through and remove dark veins. Rinse in cold water and pat dry with kitchen paper. Coat with cornflour and set aside.
Finely chop shallots or onion, bamboo shoots, ginger and garlic.
Mix sauce ingredients in a bowl.

Cooking:
Heat deep oil to very hot and reduce heat slightly.
Drop in prawns and deep-fry for 1 minute. Remove and drain. Pour off all but 3 tablespoons oil and stir-fry onions, bamboo shoots, ginger and garlic for 1 minute.
Pour in the sauce and bring to the boil. Return prawns and simmer until sauce thickens and becomes clear, about 2½ minutes.

Serving:
Sprinkle with sesame oil and finely chopped shallot.

Spiced Chicken

625 g (1¼ lb) chicken breasts
2 tablespoons poultry marinade
1 teaspoon five spices powder
4 tablespoons cornflour
2 fresh red chillies
2 shallots (or 1 small onion)
4 slices fresh ginger
2 cloves garlic
deep-frying oil
Sauce:
½ cup water
1 teaspoon chicken stock powder
1 tablespoon dark soy sauce
1 tablespoon dry sherry
½ teaspoon white vinegar
1 teaspoon sugar
1 teaspoon sesame oil
2 teaspoons cornflour
pinch each of five spices powder and white pepper

Preparation:
Skin chicken, remove any bones and cut into bite-sized cubes. Season with marinade and five-spices powder and mix well. Leave for 20 minutes.
Cut chillies and shallots into long shreds. Mince ginger and garlic.
Mix sauce ingredients in a bowl.
Place chicken in a plastic bag with cornflour and shake vigorously to thickly coat with the flour.

Cooking:
Heat deep oil to very hot, reduce heat and fry chicken until cooked through and lightly coloured, about 3 minutes. Lift out and drain well.
In another pan heat 3 tablespoons of the oil and stir-fry chillies, shallots, ginger and garlic for 1 minute. Remove. Pour in the sauce and bring to the boil.
Return chicken and the fried vegetables and stir on high heat until sauce thickens.

Serving:
Arrange on a serving plate, spoon on the sauce and garnish with fresh coriander.

Stir-Fried Chicken with Beanshoots and Hot Peppers

375 g (¾ lb) chicken, boneless
1½ tablespoons poultry marinade
2 egg whites
2 teaspoons cornflour
375 g (¾ lb) fresh beanshoots
1-2 fresh red chillies
deep-frying oil
Sauce:
4 tablespoons water
1 teaspoon chicken stock powder
1 teaspoon dry sherry
½ teaspoon sugar
½ teaspoon cornflour
pinch each of salt and white pepper

Preparation:
Skin well-chilled chicken and cut into thin slices, then into fine shreds. Season with marinade and leave for 10 minutes, then add lightly beaten egg whites and cornflour and leave for 10 more minutes.
Rinse beanshoots and remove roots and pods. Shred chillies. Mix sauce ingredients in a bowl.

Cooking:
Heat deep oil in a wok or saucepan to moderately hot and deep-fry chicken until white, about 1 minute. Remove and keep warm.
Pour off all but 3 tablespoons oil and fry beanshoots with shredded chillies for 1½-2 minutes, until just softened. Return chicken and pour in the sauce. Bring to the boil, stirring constantly.
Simmer until sauce thickens.

Serving:
Garnish the dish with sliced cucumber and tomato.

Westlake Fish, page 68 ▶

Szechwan Diced Chicken

375 g (¾ lb) chicken, boneless
1½ tablespoons poultry marinade
2 teaspoons cornflour
1 green pepper
1 fresh red chilli
6 dried black mushrooms, soaked
90 g (3 oz) canned bamboo shoots, drained
3 shallots (or 1 medium onion)
4 cloves garlic
4 slices fresh ginger
4 tablespoons vegetable oil
Sauce:
¼ cup water
¼ teaspoon chicken stock powder
1 tablespoon dark soy sauce
2 teaspoons Worcester sauce
2 tablespoons Hoisin or barbecue sauce
1 teaspoon chilli oil or chilli sauce
2 teaspoons dry sherry
1 tablespoon sugar
1 teaspoon sesame oil
1 teaspoon cornflour
pinch of white pepper

Preparation:
Cut well-chilled chicken into 1.25cm (½″) dice. Season with marinade and cornflour and leave for 20 minutes. Cut green pepper and chilli into fine dice. Squeeze water from mushrooms, remove stems, and cut into small dice. Dice bamboo shoots and finely chop shallots or onion, garlic and ginger. Mix sauce ingredients in a bowl.

Cooking:
Heat oil in a wok and stir-fry diced chicken with garlic until half cooked, about 1½ minutes. Lift out and keep warm. Add vegetables and stir-fry for 2-3 minutes, then return chicken and pour in the sauce. Bring to the boil.
Simmer, stirring constantly, until sauce thickens.

Serving:
Spoon onto a serving plate and sprinkle with sesame oil and white pepper. Garnish with shredded red or green chilli.

"Ma Po" Minced Pork with Beancurd

4 squares soft beancurd
½ teaspoon salt
375 g (¾ lb) lean pork
2 tablespoons pork marinade
2 teaspoons cornflour
¾ teaspoon sesame oil (optional)
1 shallot
3 cloves garlic
45 g (1½ oz) frozen green peas
4 tablespoons oil
Sauce:
⅓ cup water
1 teaspoon chicken or beef stock powder
2½ teaspoons garlic and chilli sauce
1 teaspoon sugar
1 teaspoon sesame oil
1 teaspoon cornflour
pinch each of salt and white pepper

Preparation:
Cut beancurd into small dice and place in a dish. Sprinkle with salt.
Mince or very finely chop the pork and season with marinade, cornflour and sesame oil, if used, and leave for 20 minutes. Slice shallot and garlic.
Thaw peas in boiling water. Drain.
Mix sauce ingredients in a bowl.

Cooking:
Heat oil in a wok and stir-fry half the garlic for ½ minute, then add shallot and beancurd and fry, turning only once, for 1½ minutes on moderately high heat. Lift out, drain and keep warm.
Reheat the oil and add remaining garlic. Stir-fry pork until colour changes, about 1½ minutes.
Pour in the sauce and bring to the boil. Simmer for 7-8 minutes, then return beancurd and gently heat through.

Serving:
Sprinkle with sesame oil and garnish with finely chopped fresh coriander or shallots.

Twice-Cooked Garlic Pork

625g (1¼ lb) pork tenderloin
2 tablespoons vegetable oil
1 whole star anise
1 teaspoon brown peppercorns (optional)
1 teaspoon five spices powder
4 shallots (or 1 medium onion)
8 cloves garlic
½ each red and green peppers
3 dried black mushrooms, soaked
4-5 tablespoons vegetable oil
Sauce:
¼ cup water
½ teaspoon chicken stock powder
2 tablespoons dark soy sauce
2 tablespoons Hoisin sauce or sweet bean
  paste
2 teaspoons dry sherry
½ teaspoon salt
1½ teaspoons sugar
1 teaspoon sesame oil
1 teaspoon cornflour
pinch of white pepper

Preparation:
Place pork on a fireproof plate and rub in the 2 tablespoons oil. Scatter on broken star anise and peppercorns, lightly ground, and rub in the five spices powder.
Coarsely chop shallots or onion. Slice garlic, lengthways. Cut peppers into 2cm (¾″) squares.
Squeeze water from mushrooms, remove stems and slice caps thinly. Mix sauce ingredients in a bowl.

Cooking:
Set pork over boiling water and steam for 30 minutes. Lift out and leave to cool, then cut into thin slices.
Drop peppers into boiling water to blanch for 20 seconds. Drain and splash with cold water to brighten colour. Drain again. Heat oil in a wok and stir-fry garlic on moderately high heat for a few seconds. Add shallot or onion and stir-fry for 1 minute.
Add the sliced pork and stir-fry until well browned. Add peppers and mushrooms and stir over high heat for about ½ minute.
Pour in the sauce and bring to the boil. Simmer, stirring, until the sauce thickens and glazes the meat.

Serving:
Arrange sliced pork on a plate with peppers, onions and mushrooms. Sprinkle with sesame oil and white pepper.

Simmered Pork

1 kg (2 lb) pork tenderloin
3 tablespoons lard or vegetable oil
¾ cup water
¾ cup dark soy sauce
½ cup dry sherry
90 g (3 oz) brown sugar or honey
8 slices fresh ginger
4 shallots (or 1 medium onion)
1 tablespoon cornflour

Preparation:
Trim pork and cut into 5cm (2") chunks.
Place in a heavy based saucepan or casserole
with lard or oil, water, soy sauce, sherry and
brown sugar.
Shred ginger and shallots and add to the
pan.

Cooking:
Bring to the boil, reduce heat to very low
and simmer until pork is absolutely tender,
about 2¼ hours. Mix cornflour with a little
cold water and stir into the sauce to thicken.
Skim off excess oil.

Serving:
Garnish with finely chopped fresh coriander
and serve with white rice.

Barbecued Spareribs

750 g (1½ lb) lean pork spareribs
4 tablespoons light soy sauce
3 tablespoons brown sugar or honey
1 teaspoon five spices powder
Seasoning:
1 tablespoon red beancurd cheese, mashed
2 tablespoons Hoisin sauce or sweet bean
    paste
1½ tablespoons smooth peanut paste
1½ teaspoons sugar

Preparation:
Divide ribs and trim well. Place in a pan and
pour on soy sauce, honey and five-spices
powder. Add enough water to just cover.
Mix seasoning ingredients separately,
adding a little vegetable oil if the mixture is
very thick.

Cooking:
Boil the ribs in the flavourings, partially
covered, until the liquid has evaporated and
ribs are half cooked. Leave to cool, then
smear thickly with the seasoning paste and
place on a well-oiled baking tray.
Bake on the upper shelf of a preheated hot
oven until the ribs are beginning to crisp.
Turn and cook other side. Brush with any
remaining seasoning and a little oil and cook
until well done and very crisp.

Serving:
Arrange on a plate lined with paper napkins
and serve with bowls of Hoisin sauce and
spicy salt.

Szechwan Stewed Beef

750 g (1½ lb) lean flank beef
4 shallots (or 1 large onion)
6 slices fresh ginger
1 whole star anise
1 dried tangerine peel (or 1 fresh orange
    peel)
3 cloves garlic
1 tablespoon brown peppercorns (or 1
    teaspoon black peppercorns)
4 tablespoons vegetable oil
Sauce:
¾ cup dark soy sauce
3 tablespoons sweet bean paste or Hoisin
    sauce
2 tablespoons dry sherry
1½ tablespoons sugar
1 tablespoon cornflour

Preparation:
Trim meat and cut into 5cm (2") chunks.
Slice shallots or onion and place in a large
saucepan with meat, ginger, broken star
anise and chopped tangerine peel. Slice
garlic and lightly crush peppercorns. Mix
sauce ingredients in a bowl.

Cooking:
Cover meat with cold water and bring to the
boil. Reduce heat and simmer until tender,
about 2½ hours.
Remove from the stock and drain well, then
cut or break into smaller pieces. Set aside.
Strain stock back into the pan and add the
pre-mixed sauce. Bring to the boil and
simmer on low heat for about 15 minutes.
Heat oil in a wok and fry garlic and
peppercorns on moderately high heat for ½
minute.
Add the meat and stir-fry on high heat until
well coloured. Return to the stock with
garlic and pepper and simmer for about 30
minutes more.

Serving:
Transfer to a deep dish and serve with
steamed white rice.

Bean Salad, page 62; Chilli Beef with Vegetables, page 76 ▶

Chilli Beef with Vegetables

375 g (¾ lb) fillet or frying steak
3 tablespoons meat marinade
2 teaspoons cornflour
½ teaspoon bicarbonate of soda
2 stalks celery
1 medium carrot
45 g (1½ oz) canned bamboo shoots, drained
1 large onion
125 g (¼ lb) fresh beanshoots
90 g (3 oz) long or green beans
3 slices fresh ginger
4 tablespoons vegetable oil
Seasoning:
2 tablespoons light soy sauce
2 teaspoons hot bean paste or chilli sauce
1 tablespoon dry sherry
1 teaspoon sugar

Preparation:
Slice well-chilled beef very thinly across the grain, then into narrow strips. Season with marinade, cornflour and bicarbonate of soda and leave for 30 minutes.
Cut celery, carrot and bamboo shoots into matchstick pieces. Thinly slice onion. Rinse beanshoots and drain. Cut beans into pieces the same length as the other vegetables. Shred ginger.
Mix seasonings in a bowl.

Cooking:
Parboil celery, carrots and beans in slightly salted water for 1 minute. Drain well.
Heat oil in a wok and stir-fry drained beef on high heat until very well coloured and slightly dry. Lift out and set aside. Add vegetables, except beanshoots, and ginger and stir-fry for 1½ minutes, then remove. Pour in seasoning and any remaining marinade and return beef. Stir on high heat until the liquid dries up, then return vegetables with beanshoots.
Continue to stir-fry until the dish is completely dry and the vegetables tender. Meat should be quite crisp.

Serving:
Serve with a small dish of sliced chillies or chilli sauce, and garnish with cucumber and pineapple slices.

Garlic Steaks ▶

625 g (1¼ lb) fillet steak
4 tablespoons meat marinade
2 teaspoons cornflour
6 cloves garlic
4 shallots (or 1 large onion)
4 tablespoons vegetable oil
Seasoning:
¼ cup water
2 tablespoons dark soy sauce
2 tablespoons oyster sauce
1 teaspoon sugar

Preparation:
Slice well-chilled steak across the grain into 1cm (¼") escalopes. Season with marinade and cornflour and leave for 45 minutes.
Slice garlic and shallots or onion.
Mix seasoning ingredients in a bowl.

Cooking:
Heat oil in a wok and fry drained steaks with garlic for ½-¾ minute on each side on very high heat. Lift out.
Fry shallots or onion until softened.
Pour in the pre-mixed seasonings with any remaining marinade and bring to the boil. Add beef, reduce heat and simmer until sauce thickens and meat is just cooked through. It should ideally be very rare.

Serving:
Arrange steaks on a serving plate and add onion and garlic.
Garnish with thinly sliced red chilli.

Sweet and Sour Cabbage Salad ▶

750 g (1½ lb) Chinese or celery cabbage
8 slices fresh ginger
2 fresh red chillies
2 teaspoons brown or black peppercorns
¾ cup white vinegar
60 g (2 oz) sugar
1½ teaspoons salt
1 tablespoon sesame oil
¼ cup vegetable oil

Preparation:
Discard outer leaves and hard stems of cabbage and shred finely. Shred ginger and chillies.
Mix vinegar with sugar and salt.

Cooking:
Heat oil in a wok and fry peppercorns for 1 minute. Add cabbage and ginger with chillies and stir-fry until the cabbage has softened slightly, about 4 minutes. Pour in the vinegar mixture and bring to the boil. Remove from the heat and leave to marinate until cool.

Serving:
Stir in sesame oil and chill slightly before serving.

Note:
Prepare this salad at least 3 hours in advance for maximum flavour.

Quick Fry Spinach ▶

750 g (1½ lb) fresh spinach
3 cloves garlic
2 tablespoons lard or vegetable oil
1 slice ham (or 3 rashers streaky bacon)
1 teaspoon sugar
1 tablespoon dry sherry
1 tablespoon water
¼ teaspoon chicken stock powder
2 teaspoons light soy sauce
1 teaspoon sesame oil
salt

Preparation:
Wash spinach three or four times in cold water and drain well. Remove stems. Chop garlic and ham or bacon finely.

Cooking:
Heat lard or vegetable oil and fry ham or bacon until crisp. Remove from pan and set aside.
Add chopped garlic and stir-fry on high heat for ½ minute. Add the spinach and sprinkle on sugar and dry sherry. Stir-fry for 1 minute on high heat, then add the water, chicken stock powder, and soy sauce. Mix well, cover and cook on moderate heat until tender, about 5 minutes. Shake pan from time to time to turn vegetables. Add salt to taste.

Serving:
Transfer to a serving dish and stir in the sesame oil. Garnish with crisp ham or bacon.

Note:
Snow peas, beanshoots, Chinese cabbage or Chinese green vegetables can be cooked in this way. They should be tender, but retaining crispness.

Shrimps in Tomato Sauce on Popped Rice Cakes

250 g (½ lb) glutinous white rice
375 g (¾ lb) raw baby shrimps, peeled
125 g (¼ lb) lean pork or chicken breast
1 tablespoon pork or poultry marinade
1 teaspoon cornflour
6 dried black mushrooms, soaked
60 g (2 oz) frozen green peas
3 shallots (or 1 medium onion)
5 slices fresh ginger
6 cloves garlic
1 fresh red chilli (optional)
deep-frying oil
Sauce:
2½ cups water
1 tablespoon chicken stock powder
1 tablespoon dark soy sauce
2 tablespoons tomato paste
1-1½ teaspoons garlic and chilli sauce
  (optional)
2 tablespoons white vinegar
1½ tablespoons sugar
2 teaspoons sesame oil
1 tablespoon cornflour
pinch of white pepper

Preparation:
Pour rice into a saucepan and cover with water to about 5cm (2″) above the level of the rice. Bring to the boil, cover tightly and cook on very low heat until the water is completely absorbed, then continue to cook until the rice has totally dried out, about 1½ hours. If the cooker will not regulate to very low, place in a low oven once the water has been completely absorbed.
Prise from the bottom of the pan with a spatula and break into squares. If not completely dry, leave in the oven for a further ½-1 hour.
Rinse shrimps in cold water and pat dry with kitchen paper. Finely shred chilled pork or chicken, season with marinade and cornflour and leave for 10 minutes.
Squeeze water from mushrooms, remove stems and slice finely. Thaw peas in boiling water. Drain well.
Shred shallots or thinly slice onion.
Finely chop ginger, garlic and chilli.
Mix sauce ingredients in a saucepan.

Cooking:
Bring sauce to the boil and simmer for at least 5 minutes, stirring frequently. Keep hot.
Heat deep oil to very hot and deep-fry the rice cakes to a deep golden brown. Lift out and drain well. Place in a soup tureen or serving bowl.
Deep-fry shrimps for ½ minute, then set aside.
Pour off all but 4 tablespoons oil and stir-fry pork or chicken until white, about 1½ minutes. Add vegetables and stir-fry for a further 1 minute on high heat.
Return shrimps and stir-fry briefly, then pour in the sauce and bring to the boil.

Serving:
Pour the shrimp sauce over the popped rice cakes at the table.

Combination Chow Mein

4-5 bundles (about 185 g/6 oz) thin egg
    noodles
125 g (¼ lb) Chinese roast pork
185 g (6 oz) chicken breasts
2 tablespoons poultry marinade
2 teaspoons cornflour
125 g (¼ lb) raw baby shrimps, peeled
2 teaspoons seafood marinade
125 g (¼ lb) fresh beanshoots
125 g (¼ lb) Chinese cabbage or other green
    vegetables
1 clove garlic
vegetable oil
Sauce:
½ cup water
1 teaspoon chicken stock powder
1 tablespoon light soy sauce
1 teaspoon salt
1 teaspoon cornflour
pinch each of sugar and white pepper

Preparation:
Soak noodles in hot water for 10 minutes
until bundles loosen. Pull apart, drain well
and spread on a tray to partially dry.
Thinly slice roast pork and cut into strips.
Shred chilled chicken and season with
marinade and cornflour, leave for 10
minutes.
Rinse shrimp, dry with kitchen paper and
season with marinade, leave for 7-8 minutes.
Rinse beanshoots and drain well. Shred
cabbage. Crush garlic. Mix sauce
ingredients in a bowl.

Cooking:
Heat about 3 tablespoons oil in a large wok
and fry noodles on both sides until the edges
are crisp. Lift out in one piece and place on a
serving plate. Keep warm.
Add a little more oil to the pan and stir-fry
chicken until white, about 1 minute on high
heat. Add shrimps and cook together for 1½
minutes. Lift out and set aside.
Add sliced pork with crushed garlic and stir-
fry lightly, then set aside also.
Add about 2 tablespoons oil to the pan and
fry vegetables until softened, about 2
minutes. Pour in the sauce and bring to the
boil.
Return meats and stir on moderate heat
until sauce thickens.

Serving:
Spoon meat and vegetables over the noodles
and pour on the sauce. Garnish with
shredded omelette and dry-fried onion.

Dried-Fried Onion

1 large onion
deep-frying oil

Thinly slice onion and pat hard between
several layers of kitchen paper to extract
most of the moisture.
Drop into very hot deep oil and fry until
crisp and dark. Drain well and leave to cool.
Store in a screw-top jar until needed.

Beef on Crisp Noodles

250 g (½ lb) frying or fillet steak
2½ tablespoons meat marinade
1 teaspoon cornflour
¼ teaspoon bicarbonate of soda (optional)
1 medium carrot
1 green pepper
1 large onion
3 slices fresh ginger
2 cloves garlic
90 g (3 oz) rice stick noodles
deep-frying oil
Sauce:
¾ cup beef stock or consomme
2 teaspoons dark soy sauce
2 tablespoons oyster sauce
1-1½ teaspoons hot bean paste
1 teaspoon sugar
½ teaspoon sesame oil
1 teaspoon cornflour

Preparation:
Slice well-chilled beef very thinly across the
grain, then cut into fine shreds. Place in a
bowl with marinade, cornflour and
bicarbonate of soda, if used. Mix well and
leave for 30 minutes.
Cut carrot and pepper into long shreds.
Thinly slice onion. Shred ginger and chop
onion.
Mix sauce ingredients in a bowl.

Cooking:
Heat deep oil to very hot and drop in
handfuls of broken rice stick noodles. Cook
until they expand and float to the surface,
but remove before they begin to colour.
Drain and place on a serving plate.
Pour off all but 4 tablespoons oil and fry
carrot, pepper and onion for 1½ minutes.
Lift out.
Add drained beef with ginger and garlic and
stir-fry on high heat for 1½ minutes. Pour in
the sauce and any remaining marinade and
return vegetables. Bring sauce to the boil
and simmer, stirring, until it thickens and
becomes clear.

Serving:
Spoon meat and vegetables over the noodles
and add the sauce. Garnish with shredded
red chilli.

Shrimps in Tomato Sauce on Popped Rice Cakes, page 78▶

Dim Sims and Snacks

Not since the introduction several decades ago of the heavy, minced pork filled "Dim Sim" and its crisp and flavourful companion the "Chicko Roll" has there been such an interest in one particular aspect of this diverse cuisine.

The range of snacks in Chinese cooking is infinite, in fact limited only by the characteristic of the food itself — which requires that it be no more than a couple of mouthfuls, and preferably be "finger food" — and by the chef's imagination.

Today, increasingly, dim sims appear in many forms in restaurant menus, where they are served as an appetiser or snack, just as they were originally intended when they were devised by Sung Dynasty chefs centuries ago.

Meat filled pastries, varying from crisp fried to tender steamed, from small bowls of braised meats to slices of roasted poultry, beef or pork all come under the category of Chinese snacks, more accurately termed 'Dim Sum' which translates loosely as "heart warmers."

Our small selection is composed of the popular and better known snacks which include Spring Rolls, Wonton and Pork Dim Sims.

Serve them as a snack, a starter or a between courses filler while you prepare the next dishes.

Golden Shrimp Balls ▶

(Makes 12 sticks)
625 g (1¼ lb) raw baby shrimps, peeled
45 g (1½ oz) pork fat
1 tablespoon seafood marinade
¾ teaspoon salt
1 teaspoon sugar
2 egg whites
2 tablespoons cornflour
pinch of white pepper
deep-frying oil
bamboo skewers or satay sticks

Preparation:
Rinse shrimps well and pat dry with kitchen paper. Pound to a smooth paste. Very finely chop, or mince, the fat pork.
Mix all ingredients together, kneading until smooth and well blended.
To form into balls, take a handful of the mixture and squeeze out between curled forefinger and thumb. Scoop off small balls with a spoon and drop into cold water.

Cooking:
Bring a large saucepan of water to the boil. Add a little salt and drop in the shrimp balls, several at a time to keep the water bubbling. Boil until they rise to the surface, then cook for about 2 more minutes. Lift out and drain well.
Heat deep oil to very hot in a wok or sauce pan and deep-fry shrimp balls to a light golden colour. Drain.

Serving:
Thread several onto each bamboo skewer or satay stick and arrange on a serving plate lined with fresh lettuce.
Serve with soy sauce or sweet chilli sauce.

Prawn Toast

(Makes 12)
8 slices fresh white bread
12 medium raw prawns, in shells
185 g (6 oz) raw baby shrimps, peeled
3 egg whites
1 tablespoon plain flour
½ shallot
2 slices fresh ginger
1 teaspoon lemon juice
1 teaspoon salt
½ teaspoon white pepper
½ teaspoon dry mustard
1 tablespoon cornflour
1 egg
2 tablespoons dry white breadcrumbs
deep-frying oil

Preparation:
Remove crusts from 6 slices of bread and cut each slice in halves. Set aside.
Grind the remaining two slices in a blender to make fine crumbs.
Peel prawns, leaving tails intact. Slit down the centre backs, cutting almost through. Remove dark veins. Press flat, and bat with the flat side of a cleaver to flatten and soften. Finely mince or pound the shrimps and mix with the fresh breadcrumbs, well beaten egg whites and flour. Add minced shallot and ginger and season with lemon juice, salt, white pepper and mustard. Mix very well. Dampen each piece of bread slightly with water and place one of the flattened prawns on top, with tail protruding over the end. Coat thickly with shrimp paste and smooth over. Coat lightly with cornflour, then brush with beaten egg. Cover with breadcrumbs.

Cooking:
Heat deep oil to moderately hot and deep-fry the prawn toasts, several at a time, for about 2 minutes. They should be golden brown.
Lift out and drain well.

Serving:
Arrange on a plate and garnish with fresh coriander and sliced lemon.

Deep-Fried Wontons (top), page 84 ▶

Spring Rolls

(Makes 25)
Wrappers:
1 pack of 25 frozen spring roll wrappers
Filling:
375 g (¾ lb) lean pork
½ teaspoon salt
1 teaspoon cornflour
4 dried black mushrooms, soaked
2 shallots
45 g (1½ oz) canned bamboo shoots, drained
125 g (¼ lb) Chinese cabbage
deep-frying oil
Seasoning:
2 tablespoons water
½ teaspoon chicken stock powder
1 tablespoon light soy sauce
2 teaspoons dry sherry
1½ teaspoons sugar
1 tablespoon vegetable oil
1 teaspoon cornflour

Preparation:
Thaw spring roll wrappers, then cover with a damp cloth. Slice well-chilled pork thinly across the grain, then cut into fine shreds. Season with salt and cornflour and set aside. Squeeze water from mushrooms, remove stems and slice caps. Shred shallot, bamboo shoots and Chinese cabbage.
Mix seasonings in a bowl.

Cooking:
In a dry wok stir-fry cabbage until much of the water has been dried out. Set aside.
Add 3 tablespoons oil and when very hot stir-fry pork for 2 minutes. Add mushrooms, shallot and bamboo shoots and stir-fry for 1 more minute.
Add the cabbage and pre-mixed seasonings and stir-fry until the liquid has been absorbed. Remove from the pan and leave to cool. Place a large spoonful of the mixture towards one corner of each wrapper. Fold diagonally, tucking the lower flap and two sides in. Fold the last flap over the roll and stick down with water or a flour and water paste. In a clean pan heat deep oil until very hot, then reduce heat slightly. Deep-fry spring rolls, several at a time, to a medium golden colour. Lift out and drain well.

Serving:
Serve with dark soy sauce, Worcester sauce or sweet and sour sauce.

Pork Dim Sims

(Makes 30)
Wrappers:
2½ cups plain flour
½ cup boiling water
¼ cup cold water
1 tablespoon vegetable oil
Filling:
500 g (1 lb) finely minced lean pork
60 g (2 oz) raw baby shrimps, peeled
45 g (1½ oz) canned bamboo shoots, drained
3 shallots (or 1 medium onion)
deep-frying oil
Seasoning:
2 teaspoons light soy sauce
2 teaspoons dry sherry
1 teaspoon salt
2 teaspoons sugar
¼ teaspoon black pepper
2 teaspoons sesame oil
1 tablespoon cornflour

Preparation:
Sift flour into a mixing bowl and make a well in the centre. Pour in boiling water and mix loosely, then add the cold water and oil and work until well blended.
Knead for 5 minutes until very smooth and pliable. Roll into a thin long sausage shape and cut into 30 pieces. Cover with a damp cloth.
Pound the minced pork in a mortar, or pass through an electric blender, to make extra-smooth. Finely dice shrimps, bamboo shoots and shallots and add to the pork. Blend in the seasoning ingredients and mix well.
Flatten each piece of dough into thin discs about 6cm (2½") in diameter, using a rolling pin on a floured board.
Place a generous spoonful of the mixture in the centre of each wrapper and pull up the sides to make dumplings. The pastry should just touch at the top.

Cooking:
Arrange the prepared dim sims in large greased bamboo steaming baskets and steam over high heat, covered for 7-8 minutes. When ready to serve, drop into very hot deep oil and fry to a light golden brown. Drain well.

Serving:
Serve with soy or sweet and sour sauce.

Note:
They may be served steamed instead of deep fried, with a dip of soy sauce and shredded young ginger.

Deep-Fried Wontons

(Makes 25)
Wrappers:
1 pack of 25 frozen spring roll wrappers (or 25 pieces edible rice paper)
Filling:
250 g (½ lb) pork tenderloin or boneless chicken
250 g (½ lb) raw baby shrimps
30 g (1 oz) pork fat (optional)
30 g (1 oz) canned water chestnuts or bamboo shoots, drained
2 tablespoons chopped fresh coriander
1 shallot
1 teaspoon salt
1 teaspoon sugar
¼ teaspoon white pepper
2 teaspoons cornflour
deep-frying oil

Preparation:
Thaw spring roll wrappers, if used, then cover with a damp cloth and set aside.
Very finely mince or chop pork or chicken. Peel shrimps, rinse well and pat dry with kitchen paper. Chop shrimps and pork fat, if used, very finely and mix with the meat. Mince or finely dice water chestnuts or bamboo shoots, and shallot.
Mix with the meat and shrimps and season with coriander, salt, sugar, white pepper and cornflour. Blend together well.
Place a spoonful of the mixture in the centre of each wrapper and gather up the sides. Press around the filling to form into a ball shapes in the centre, pinching the wrappers together to form a waist with the edges of the wrapper fanning out above.

Cooking:
Heat deep oil to moderately hot in a wok or deep saucepan. Drop in wontons, several at a time, to deep-fry to a light golden colour, about 3 minutes.
Lift out and drain well.

Serving:
Arrange on a plate and serve with a sweet and sour sauce.

Spring Rolls (above) ▶

Fried Crab Claws

12 crab pincers
625 g (1¼ lb) raw baby shrimps, peeled
1 tablespoon lemon juice
½ teaspoon salt
¼ teaspoon white pepper
½ teaspoon dry mustard
1 tablespoon water
2 egg whites
1 egg
cornflour
white sesame seeds
deep-frying oil

Preparation:
Break away the main part of the shell, leaving one point of the pincer attached to the crabmeat.

Pound baby shrimps to a paste, seasoning with lemon juice, salt, pepper and mustard. Add in water and egg whites and about 1 tablespoon cornflour to bind. Work to a smooth paste.

Divide into 12 parts and mould each portion around one of the prepared pincers, leaving the tip of the pincer shell exposed.

Smooth into ball shapes and coat lightly with cornflour. Brush with beaten egg and dip the end into sesame seeds. Coat again with cornflour.

Cooking:
Heat deep oil to moderately hot and deep-fry, several at a time, until light gold in colour, about 3 minutes. Lift out and drain well.

Serving:
Arrange on a plate with lemon wedges and sprigs of parsley.

Soups

The Chinese regard soup as an essential element to a balanced meal. It is, unlike the Western tradition, served mid-way in a meal rather than at the beginning. Its main function is to cleanse and refresh the palate, so that the following dishes can be fully appreciated. And for this reason, it is generally served either after a strongly flavoured dish, or prior to an "important" dish, such as a whole fish or bird which may be served as the highlight of the meal.

Additionally the soup stock is regarded as being ultimately pure and health giving. A majority of Chinese soups have a clear stock base, generally made from chicken carcases by slow simmering with water and a minimum of seasonings. Clear soups like the Mushroom Soup recipe given here, obtain their flavour from the main ingredient itself, unadulterated, and rely on long double-boiling to extract the full flavour.

Popular soups like the Combination Long Soup and Wonton Soup with Meat and Vegetables have a hearty content of meats, seafoods and pasta and make virtually a meal in themselves.

Golden Sweetcorn Soup

250 g (½ lb) chicken, boneless
375 g (¾ lb) can cream-style sweetcorn
5 cups water
1¾ tablespoons chicken stock powder
1 teaspoon salt
1 heaped tablespoon cornflour
1 shallot
2 egg whites
light soy sauce

Preparation:
Mince or finely chop chicken.
Pour sweetcorn and water into a saucepan and add salt and cornflour. Mix well.
Finely chop shallot and beat egg whites.

Cooking:
Being stock and sweetcorn mixture to the boil, stirring until it begins to thicken. Add chicken and boil for at least 5 minutes, then stir in the shallot and remove from the heat. Pour in egg whites and leave until the egg sets in white threads in the soup, then add soy sauce to taste and stir well. Reheat briefly.

Serving:
Pour into a soup tureen and garnish with fresh coriander.

Clear Mushroom Soup

15 dried black mushrooms, soaked
6 cups water
1 tablespoon light soy sauce
2 teaspoons dry sherry
pinch each of salt, white pepper and
  bicarbonate of soda

Preparation:
Squeeze water from mushrooms and remove stems. Place in a double-boiler with water.

Cooking:
Bring to the boil. Add soy sauce, sherry, salt, pepper and soda and double-boil for 2½ hours, on moderate heat.

Serving:
Transfer to a soup tureen and garnish with shredded fresh ginger.

Winter Melon Soup ▶

500 g (1 lb) canned winter melon, drained
90 g (3 oz) chicken, boneless
90 g (3 oz) ham or bacon
2 shallots (or 1 small onion)
3 dried black mushrooms, soaked
60 g (2 oz) frozen green peas
60 g (2 oz) canned small button mushrooms,
  drained
5 cups water
1 tablespoon chicken stock powder
2-3 teaspoons light soy sauce
1 teaspoon sesame oil (optional)
4 kg (8 lb) water melon (optional)

Preparation:
Shred chicken and bacon. Finely chop shallots.
Squeeze water from mushrooms, remove stems and slice. Thaw peas in boiling water. Remove top of water melon, if using, and scoop out the seeds. Remove flesh with a melon baller and chill to serve as dessert. Rinse out the hollowed shell and fill with salted water.

Cooking:
Set the water melon shell in a steamer and cook over boiling water for about 45 minutes. Remove and drain. Set in a stand or casserole which will hold it upright. Bring water to the boil and add stock and soy sauce. Simmer for 5 minutes, then add the meat and vegetables and simmer until all are tender.

Serving:
Pour into the melon shell and sprinkle on sesame oil, if used.

Note:
If water melon is unavailable, prepare the soup in the same way and serve in a soup tureen or deep serving bowl.

Combination Long Soup

185 g (6 oz) thick egg noodles (or spaghetti)
5 dried black mushrooms, soaked
60 g (2 oz) lean pork
60 g (2 oz) chicken, boneless
185 g (6 oz) Chinese or celery cabbage
1 square soft beancurd (or 45 g/1½ oz
button mushrooms)
2 slices fresh ginger
6 cups water
2 tablespoons chicken stock powder
1 tablespoon light soy sauce
1 tablespoon dry sherry
1 teaspoon sesame oil
2 tablespoons vegetable oil
pinch each of sugar, salt and white pepper

Preparation:
Soak noodles in boiling water to soften, about 12 minutes, then drain well. If using spaghetti, simmer in slightly salted water for 10 minutes. Drain.
Squeeze water from mushrooms, remove stems and slice thinly. Slice chilled pork and chicken, then cut into fine shreds. Wash cabbage and cut into 5cm (2″) squares, discarding hard stems. Dice beancurd and shred ginger.

Cooking:
Bring water to the boil in a large saucepan and add stock powder, soy sauce, sherry and seasonings.
Reduce heat and simmer for 10 minutes. Heat oil in a wok and stir-fry pork and chicken shreds for 1½ minutes. Add to the soup with ginger. Simmer for about 10 minutes, then add noodles and cook until just tender.
Add black mushrooms and cabbage and simmer until softened, then just before serving add in diced beancurd or button mushrooms and heat through.

Serving:
Season with additional soy sauce and white pepper and garnish with fresh coriander.

Chicken, Vegetable and Egg Soup

250 g (½ lb) chicken, boneless
8 dried black mushrooms, soaked
185 g (6oz) fresh spinach
1 shallot
3 slices fresh ginger
6 cups water
2 tablespoons chicken stock powder
1 tablespoon dry sherry
½ teaspoon salt
3 eggs

Preparation:
Skin chicken and cut into 2cm (¾") cubes.
Squeeze water from mushrooms, remove
stems and leave caps whole. Wash spinach
and remove stems.
Cut shallot into 2cm (¾") pieces.
Place chicken, mushrooms, onion and
ginger in a double-boiler with water, stock
powder, sherry and salt.

Cooking:
Bring to the boil and simmer for 1½ hours,
covered. Add spinach and shallot and
simmer until tender.
Heat a wok and rub with an oiled cloth.
Pour in half the lightly beaten egg. Turn pan
to form thin omelette and cook until firm.
Turn and cook other side. Remove and leave
to cool. Cook remaining egg and cool. Shred
finely.

Serving:
Transfer soup to a tureen and add the
shredded egg. Garnish with finely chopped
shallot.

Wonton Soup with Meat and Vegetables

1 pack frozen wontons
125 g (¼ lb) lean pork
125 g (¼ lb) chicken, boneless
1½ tablespoons pork marinade
4 dried black mushrooms, soaked
30 g (1 oz) canned bamboo shoots, drained
125 g (¾ lb) Chinese cabbage or other green
    vegetable
1 small carrot
1 shallot
5 cups water
1¾ tablespoons chicken stock powder
1 tablespoon light soy sauce
1 tablespoon dry sherry
1 teaspoon sesame oil
pinch each of sugar, salt and white pepper

Preparation:
Partially thaw wontons.
Shred chilled pork and chicken and season
with marinade. Leave for 10 minutes.
Squeeze water from mushrooms, remove
stems.
Thinly slice bamboo shoots, cabbage or
green vegetables and carrot. Chop shallot.
Pour water into a large saucepan and add
stock powder.

Cooking:
Bring to the boil, add mushrooms, bamboo
shoots and carrot and simmer for 5 minutes.
Add meat and simmer for 5 minutes, then
add soy sauce, sherry, sesame oil and
seasonings. Add wonton and the vegetables
and shallot and simmer on low heat until
wontons are heated through and vegetables
tender.

Serving:
Transfer to a soup tureen and season with
additional sesame oil.

Fish Ball and Celery Soup

625 g (1¼ lb) white fish fillets
1 tablespoon seafood marinade
2 egg whites
1 tablespoon water
2-3 tablespoons cornflour
3 stalks celery
6 cups fish stock or water
1 tablespoon light soy sauce
pinch of white pepper

Preparation:
Mince fish fillets, then pound to a smooth
paste in a mortar or blender. Season with
marinade and stir in beaten egg whites,
water and cornflour. Knead to a smooth,
slightly stiff paste.
Form into balls by squeezing lumps of the
paste from the hand, between curled thumb
and forefinger. Scoop each ball off with a
spoon, and drop into cold water.
Cut celery into thin diagonal slices.

Cooking:
Bring stock to the boil (if using water, add a
little chicken stock powder to make a light
stock) and season with soy sauce and
pepper.
Drop in drained fish balls and simmer on
moderate heat for about 20 minutes. Add
sliced celery and simmer until just tender.

Serving:
Pour into a soup tureen and add seasonings
to taste.

Sweets

With the tremendous range and diversity of the Chinese cuisine, it is something of an anti-climax to learn that little attention is paid to the production of sweet dishes. What sweets they have are very few, and not highly imaginative. Instead, they prefer to finish with a piece of fresh fruit, and perhaps a minute pastry.

There are, however, variations on a theme using fruits, white fungus, bird's nest and sweet preserved nuts and seeds, such as lotus seeds. These are simply double-boiled in a sugar syrup and served hot or cold.

And sweet soups made from peanut, walnut or taro root are also served, usually hot. But the most popular is undoubtedly the Peking Toffied Apple (or Banana) which has sliced apple coated in batter and deep-fried, then coated with a sugar toffee and sesame seeds.

Sweet dishes are most often served in tea houses, to accompany a meal of "Dim Sum" snacks, or to conclude a banquet-size dinner. Rarely will anything other than fresh fruit be served with a standard family meal. This observation, however, is based on the practice of Chinese families within a Chinese community. In Australia, restaurateurs have encouraged the habit of eating some sort of icecream or fruit sweet at the end of a meal, and you might like to continue this at home when you cook.

Lychees in Syrup

1 large can lychees, well-chilled
2 tablespoons sweet liqueur (Creme de Menthe, Curacao, Grand Marnier, Cointreau)
6 scoops vanilla icecream
1 tablespoon powdered sugar
1 egg white
6 fresh cherries

Preparation:
Dip cherries into beaten egg white, then coat thickly with powdered sugar. Chill well.
Drain lychees and mix syrup with liqueur.
Place a scoop of icecream in each glass dessert dish and add several drained lychees. Pour on a serving of the syrup and top with a cherry.

Serving:
Serve well chilled.

Double-Boiled Pineapple and Pawpaw ▶

6 slices canned pineapple, drained
¾ cup pineapple juice
375 g (¾ lb) barely ripe pawpaw
6 cups hot water
150 g (5 oz) slab sugar (or white sugar to taste)
30 g (1 oz) bitter almonds

Preparation:
Place pineapple slices in a small casserole or covered fireproof dish and add pineapple juice.
Cut pawpaw into six pieces and place in another small casserole or covered fireproof dish.

Cooking:
Bring water to the boil and add crumbled slab sugar or white sugar. Stir until dissolved, then pour into the casseroles, adding more to the pawpaw, to cover.
Divide almonds between the two pots.
Place in a steamer and cook over gently boiling water for 1-1¼ hours.

Serving:
Place a piece each of pineapple and pawpaw in a dessert dish. Add several almonds and cover with the piping hot sauce. Serve hot or warm.

Almond Jelly with Fruit

2 cups milk
1 tablespoon gelatine or powdered agar agar
45 g (1½ oz) sugar
1 teaspoon almond extract
1½ cups mixed fruit cocktail in syrup, chilled
pink and green food colouring (optional)

Cooking:
Heat half the milk to boiling point and sprinkle on gelatine or agar agar. Stir until dissolved.
Dissolve sugar in remaining milk over low heat. Mix with the hot milk and add almond extract.
Divide the mixture between three bowls, colouring one a light pink, one light green and leaving one white.
Leave to set, then chill until firm.

Serving:
Cut the almond jelly into triangular or diamond-shaped pieces and arrange in small glass dessert dishes.
Top each serving with a large spoonful of the fruit cocktail and syrup. Serve chilled.

2 eating apples
2 medium bananas, ripe but firm
¾ cup plain flour
2 heaped tablespoons cornflour
2 egg whites
½ teaspoon salt
½ teaspoon bicarbonate of soda
½-¾ cup cold water
white sesame seeds
iced water
deep-frying oil
Toffee:
2 cups sugar
1¼ cups water

Preparation:
Peel apples, remove cores and cut into medium-thick slices.
Cut banana diagonally into 1.25cm (1″) slices.
Prepare a batter by mixing flour with cornflour, egg whites, salt, bicarbonate of soda and enough water to make a mixture of medium consistency. Beat well, then leave for 20 minutes.
Prepare a large bowl of iced water with extra ice cubes, and place near the cooking area.
Have a well-oiled plate and the sesame seeds in a bowl, ready near the iced water.

Cooking:
Bring sugar and water to boil in a small saucepan. Stir until sugar dissolves, then reduce heat and simmer until it turns light golden and is beginning to toffee.
Keep warm, but do not continue cooking.
Heat deep oil to moderately hot.
Dip apple and banana into the batter and deep-fry, several at a time, to a light golden brown.
Lift out one by one and dip into the prepared toffee, then sprinkle with sesame seeds.
Dip into iced water to harden toffee, then place on the oiled plate.

Serving:
When all are cooked, serve at once, with additional iced water. Dip each piece into the water to re-harden toffee.

Glossary of Ingredients

A listing of the most commonly used, and some lesser known, Chinese ingredients and their substitutes.

Bamboo Shoots:

Occasionally available fresh from Chinese food suppliers, these should be peeled and the fleshy central spear steamed or boiled until tender.

Canned bamboo shoots can be stored, after opening, in fresh water in the refrigerator. The water should be changed daily.

Select only those canned in water or brine for these recipes, as those packed in soy-based sauce have a stronger flavour.

Beancurd:

The great protein-rich meat substitute made from soy beans.

When fresh beancurd cakes are not available, there are vacuum packed and powdered types on sale in many Oriental food stores, which make acceptable substitutes.

Store beancurd cakes in a dish of fresh water in the refrigerator for up to 10 days, changing the water daily.

To make pressed beancurd, place soft beancurd cakes in a strainer lined with muslin. Cover with more cloth and add enough weight to press out much of the retained liquid.

Pressed beancurd is suitable for frying.

Bean Pastes:

There are several kinds of seasoning pastes made from preserved soy beans used in Chinese cooking.

Most common are:
Hot Bean Paste: containing a mixture of crushed soy beans, chillies and garlic and varying from hot to very hot according to the brand. Sold in small jars and cans.
Sweet Bean Paste: rich and with a salty sweetness. A thick dark brown, fairly smooth paste. Sold in jars and cans. Keeps well when opened.
Yellow Bean Paste: containing whole and crushed preserved yellow soy beans. Very salty in taste. Usually sold in cans.

Beanshoots:

Readily available fresh, they will keep for at least a week if stored in a plastic bag in the refrigerator. Rinse well before use, and remove pods and roots to improve the appearance of a dish.

Canned beanshoots lack the crispness of fresh ones, but are a reasonable substitute. Drain well, then rinse in plenty of cold water.

Black Beans, Salted:

Fermented, salted soy beans sold in small packages or in cans. They keep indefinitely. A strong, salty flavour with no suitable substitute.

Black Mushrooms, Dried:

Also known as Chinese mushrooms these wrinkled dry mushrooms have a distinct aroma. Indispensible to Chinese cooking. They must be soaked to soften in warm water for at least 30 minutes. Remove and discard stems.

Choose those which have thick caps and are a pale cream colour underneath.

Button Mushrooms:

Canned champignons. Used in many Chinese dishes.

Chinese Cabbage:

"Pak Choy", the large white-steamed, green leafed vegetable sold at most Chinese food suppliers.

Keeps well in the crisper of the refrigerator. The more expensive Celery Cabbage has a distinct flavour, though is less readily available.

Good white cabbage or other Chinese green vegetables can be substituted in most dishes.

Chinese Sausage:

Dried coarsely ground pork sausages made to a special Chinese recipe. Sold, seasonally, at Chinese food suppliers. They keep well in the refrigerator, or hanging in a food closet.

Chinese Green Vegetables:

Also known as "Choy Sum", this is a bright green stem vegetable with a highly individual taste. Substitute Chinese cabbage, silverbeet, mustard greens or broccoli.

Chow Chow, Preserved:

A mixture of radish, ginger, peppers, gourd and other vegetables in a sticky semi-sweet preserving liquid. Chinese pickles are slightly less sweet.

Sold in jars. Keep indefinitely, after opening.

Coriander, Fresh:

Also known as Chinese Parsley. A leafy herb resembling Western parsley, but with a strong, pungent aroma which cannot be substituted. If unavailable, omit in a dish or substitute other parsley as a garnish.

Cornflour:

A fine maize flour used as a thickening for most sauces and frequently in batters to give extra crispness. Wheat flour should not be used to thicken, substitute arrowroot or water chestnut flour.

Garlic and Chilli Sauce:

A strongly flavoured hot sauce made from mashed garlic, red chillies and yellow soy beans. Slightly salty in taste. Substitute hot bean paste or chilli sauce.

Ginger, Fresh:

The root of the ginger plant. Used fresh to give a distinct flavour to Chinese dishes. Powdered ginger is not a substitute, having quite different characteristics.

If unavailable, use pickled ginger, often sold in Japanese food stores.

To keep root ginger, peel and slice (or leave whole) and place in a screw top jar with dry sherry or sweetened white vinegar to cover. Young root ginger has a mild, fresh flavour. It has smooth, cream coloured skin and pink shoots. Older ginger has a wrinkled appearance and is stronger in taste and more fibrous.

Hoisin Sauce:

The Chinese equivalent of barbecue sauce, being a dark red brown soy bean based sauce with a slighly sweet taste. Substitute any good barbecue sauce.

Also served as a condiment and dip, most commonly with dishes like Peking Duck which are wrapped in pancakes.

Lotus Root:

The tubular hollowed root of the lotus plant. Occasionally available fresh, but more often sliced in cans, or dried. Used for both sweet and savoury cooking.

Canned lotus root should be drained and will keep well in the refrigerator if covered with fresh water which is changed frequently.

Soak dried lotus root until beginning to soften, then steam or boil.

Noodles:

A variety of noodles made with wheat flour, rice flour and bean flour are used in Chinese cooking. Those used in these recipes include:
Egg noodles, thin: thin strands of yellow dried noodles made with flour and egg and usually sold in "bundles." They should be soaked or gently boiled to soften before use. Use in soups and fried noodle dishes.
Egg Noodles, thick: sold fresh or dried, these resemble spaghetti which could be substituted.
Fresh noodles can be added straight to a dish, or may be briefly boiled to ensure tenderness.
Boil the dried kind in plenty of water, with a little vegetable oil and salt added.
Rice stick noodles: thin white coloured noodles made from rice flour. Most commonly deep-fried, which causes them to expand and become very crisp and light. Served also in soups.
Transparent bean thread vermicelli (noodles): glass-like noodles made from a paste of ground mung beans. Used in soups and stews and are a common element in Chinese vegetarian cooking.

Oyster Sauce:

A salty, thick brown sauce made from an extract of preserved oysters. No substitute.

Plum Sauce:

A slightly sour jam-like sauce made from plums. Used in much the same way as Hoisin sauce, as a flavouring agent and condiment.

Red Beancurd Cheese:

Cubes of beancurd preserved in a brine solution with mashed red chilli. It takes on the appearance and flavour of a strong blue cheese, except that it is red-coloured. Mashed, it is used as a flavouring agent and occasionally as a condiment or dip.
No substitute can give a similar taste.

Sesame Oil:

A dark coloured, aromatic oil made from ground sesame seeds. Used frequently in the cooking of Northern China. Its taste is distinctive and is not always agreeable. If in doubt, omit.
Sold in small bottles. Keeps indefinitely.

Shallots (Spring Onion):

Dark green leafy vegetables of the onion family, with white or purple bulbs. Either the bulb part or the whole onion may be used. If unavailable, use onion or chives. Scallions, the small purple onions, are stronger in taste, but can be substituted.

Sherry, Dry:

Used as a substitute for Chinese rice wine which is not available in unlicenced Chinese food stores.

Slab Sugar:

Brown, sometimes two-toned, compressed cakes of unrefined sugar. Substitute brown or white sugar to taste.

Snow Peas:

Flat, bright green pea pod vegetables. Seasonal, available in cooler months. Also known as Mange Tout.

Soy Sauce:

An extract of soy beans produced by distillation.
There are several types of soy sauce used in Chinese cooking.
Light soy sauce is thin and salty. Used mainly for flavouring and to add salt.
Dark soy sauce is thicker and deeper in colour and is used to add colour to a dish.

Spicy Salt:

An aromatic condiment and seasoning made by mixing heated table salt with five spices powder. For recipe, see page 60.

Spring Roll Wrappers:

Thin "skins" made from wheat flour. Sold in most Oriental provision stores frozen in packs of 25 or 50. They must be kept moist when thawed and opened or they will crumble and be unusable.

Star Anise:

A fragrant eight-pointed spice with an aroma similar to aniseed, which can be substituted.
Sold in "points," broken or whole.

Straw Mushrooms:

White or brownish mushrooms, sold in cans, with a flavour and texture similar to button mushrooms but with a slightly more musky taste.

Water Chestnuts:

Crisp white vegetable sold fresh, occasionally, or in cans. Opened, the canned variety will keep well in fresh water in the refrigerator.

Wonton Wrappers:

Small square or circular "skins" made from a special high-gluten wheat flour. Used to make wontons and various dim sims.
Sold fresh or frozen. Fresh wrappers should be kept, well wrapped in plastic film, in the refrigerator.
Thaw frozen wrappers well before using. Do not allow to dry out.

Weights And Measures

Solid measurements given in metric weight, have been converted for your convenience, into avoirdupois in each recipe.
We have used the following table of conversion:

Metric	Avoirdupois
30 g	1 oz
60 g	2 oz
90 g	3 oz
125 g	¼ lb
150 g	5 oz
185 g	6 oz
220 g	7 oz
250 g	½ lb
280 g	9 oz
310 g	10 oz
340 g	11 oz
375 g	¾ lb
410 g	13 oz
440 g	14 oz
475 g	15 oz
500 g	1 lb
625 g	1¼ lb
750 g	1½ lb
1 kg	2 lb

Liquid Measurements used throughout have been based on the standard 250 ml metric cup (and half cup, third cup and quarter cup) in place of the standard 8 fl oz cup (and half cup, third cup and quarter cup), and using the standard 20 ml metric tablespoon, 5 ml teaspoon and 2.5 ml half teaspoon. The slight difference in volume of avoirdupois-based spoon measurements is not so critical in these recipes as to suggest they should not be used.